Twayne's United States Authors Series

EDITOR OF THIS VOLUME

David J. Nordloh
Indiana University

Gertrude Atherton

TUSAS 324

GERTRUDE ATHERTON

By CHARLOTTE S. McCLURE
Georgia State University

TWAYNE PUBLISHERS
A DIVISION OF G. K. HALL & CO. BOSTON

Library of Congress Cataloging in Publication Data

McClure, Charlotte S
Gertrude Atherton.

(Twayne's United States authors series; TUSAS 324)
Bibliography: p. 155-60
Includes index.
1. Atherton, Gertrude Franklin Horn, 1857-1948
—Criticism and interpretation.
[PS1043.M3 1979] 813'.5'2 78-14208
ISBN 0-8057-7216-2

To John

Contents

About the Author

Charlotte S. McClure is assistant director of the Honors Program and assistant professor of comparative literature at Georgia State University. A graduate of Denison University with honors in English, she received the M.A. and the Ph.D. in English from the University of New Mexico. She formerly covered state and local government for newspapers in Ohio and taught in public and private schools in Albuquerque, New Mexico. She is secretary of the Women's Studies section of the South Atlantic Modern Language Association.

Her other writing on Gertrude Atherton includes a bibliographic essay, a checklist of writings by and about the California novelist, and a monograph and several articles on her western fiction. She has also written reviews of women's autobiographies and critical assessments of dissertations on Atherton, Mary Austin, Willa Cather, and Susan Glaspell.

Preface

Gertrude Atherton's work is so little known yet so varied and so extensive that it calls for a concerted effort at classification, interpretation, and evaluation. Thirty years after her death, her deserved place in the history of American literature has not been determined, in part because her novels, short stories, and nonfiction, written over a period of sixty years, have been neglected by critical and scholarly attention. Therefore, this study of the artifacts of her imagination and the details of her life, so far as now known, is a first attempt to present a comprehensive view of her biography and literary achievement.

In this study, I gather the facts, analyses, and interpretations which have been scattered in libraries, archives, and English and American journals, newspapers, and magazines to illuminate the manner of Gertrude Atherton's life, the nature and purpose of her writing. It seems important that this study present first the basic material in the author's own manner and words—even her preferred name, Mrs. Atherton—and then move to interpretation and evaluation.

In Chapter 1, I present the biographical material that is available and pertinent to the understanding of a novelist and an artist, and in particular a writer who is being rediscovered. Since Atherton's own records of the first fifty years of her life were lost in the earthquake and fire in San Francisco in 1906, the resurrection of essential biographical elements depends on her autobiography, on references and allusions in her occasional pieces and letters, and on the memories of her granddaughter, Florence Atherton Dickey of Santa Rosa, California. Limited though these are, they supply sufficient evidence to portray the experience in childhood, youth, and maturity which developed her personality and guided and shaped her imagination. In Chapter 2, I collect the author's scattered and frequently cryptic remarks on the art and craft of fiction as she understood them, and trace the development of the novelist's theory and practice of fiction and present, to a considerable extent in her own words, her ideas and opinions on them.

Because Gertrude Atherton's life and the manner and subject of her fiction were cyclical, I have divided her career into five periods and special literary topics, all of which tend to overlap. In Chapters 3 through 7, I discuss her significant novels, providing summaries of the stories, analyses of the significant elements, and estimates of the importance of the books both individual and relative to each other and to her whole achievement. I refer briefly to her apprentice work, both short stories and novels, and to her nonfiction pieces. Finally, in Chapter 8, I offer a brief summary of the critical reception of her work over sixty years as an initial attempt to define her significance for the novel, which was to her "a memoir of contemporary life in the form of fiction."

I have sought to be as inclusive of Gertrude Atherton's works as possible in order to encourage a new reading of her novels, short stories, and nonfiction. Since 1968, several reprint and microfilm companies have made some of her works available. My approach will, I hope, result in a recognition of her versatility and range. One emerges from a detailed study of her total work with respect for her place in American literature—as a Realist who dared to modify fiction according to her own insight and to her observations of the human scene.

CHARLOTTE S. MCCLURE

Georgia State University

Acknowledgments

I gratefully acknowledge permission of the following to quote from books and from unpublished biographical material:

Florence A. Dickey, Santa Rosa, California, granddaughter of Gertrude Atherton, author of an unpublished memoir of the novelist and contributor of the photograph frontispiece;

Houghton Mifflin Company for quotations from *What Is a Book? Thoughts About Writing* (1935), edited by Dale Warren;

Liveright Publishing Corporation for quotations from Gertrude Atherton's *Adventures of a Novelist* (1932).

Chronology

1857   Gertrude Franklin Horn born October 30 in San Francisco; parents, Thomas Ludovich and Gertrude Franklin Horn.

1861   Resided on her grandfather Stephen Franklin's ranch after her mother's divorce.

1866–   Educated at boarding schools in San Francisco and at
1873   St. Mary's Hall, Benicia.

1874   Studied at Sayre Institute, Kentucky.

1876   Married George Bowen Atherton, February 14, in San Francisco.

1877   Birth of George, Jr.

1878   Birth of Muriel, July 14.

1879   Wrote anonymously for the *Argonaut*; reconciliation with Grandfather Franklin; lived on Oroville, California, farm.

1881   Lived in San Francisco; active in Fortnightly Club for discussion of literature.

1882   Wrote anonymously for the *Overland Monthly* and newspapers.

1883   "The Randolphs of Redwoods: A Romance" by "Asmodeus" published in the *Argonaut*. Death of George, Jr.

1885–   Active in winter social season in San Francisco.
1886

1887   Death of husband.

1888   *What Dreams May Come*, by "Frank Lin."

1889   *Hermia Suydam*. New York correspondent for the *Argonaut*. Lived in Paris.

1890   Lived in London. Returned to San Francisco because of the death of Stephen Franklin.

1891   *A Question of Time*.

1892   "The Doomswoman" serialized in *Lippincott's*. Series on resorts for the *New York World*. "The Conquest of Doña Jacoba" in *Blackwood's*. Supernatural stories for *Vanity Fair*.

1893   *The Doomswoman.*
1894   *Before the Gringo Came* (short stories).
1895   *A Whirl Asunder.* Lived in England.
1897   *Patience Sparhawk and Her Times. His Fortunate Grace.*
1898   *American Wives and English Husbands. The Californians. The Valiant Runaways.* Met Lady Colin Campbell and Henry James.
1899   *A Daughter of the Vine.* Studied the United States Senate for *Senator North.*
1900   *Senator North.*
1901   *The Aristocrats* published anonymously.
1902   *The Conqueror. The Splendid Idle Forties* (short stories).
1903   *A Few of Hamilton's Letters.*
1904   *Rulers of Kings.*
1905   *The Bell in the Fog and Other Stories. The Traveling Thirds.*
1906   Lost manuscripts, letters, and personal papers in earthquake and fire in San Francisco.
1907   *Ancestors.*
1908   *The Gorgeous Isle.*
1909   Met Minnie Maddern Fiske, well-known American actress.
1910   *Tower of Ivory.*
1911   Traveled with Mrs. Fiske. Studied British suffrage and feminism in England.
1912   *Julia France and Her Times.*
1914   *Perch of the Devil. California, An Intimate History.*
1915   *Before the Gringo Came: Rezánov* and *The Doomswoman.*
1916   *Mrs. Balfame, A Novel. Life in the War Zone* (pamphlet).
1917   *The Living Present.*
1918   *The White Morning.*
1919   *The Avalanche, A Mystery Story. Transplanted.*
1921   *The Sisters-in-Law.*
1922   *Sleeping Fires.* Underwent reactivation treatments.
1923   *Black Oxen.* Appeared at hearings on censorship before the New York State Legislature.
1924   Met Gertrude Stein.
1925   *The Crystal Cup.*

Chronology

1927   *The Immortal Marriage. California, An Intimate History* (revised).

1928   *The Jealous Gods.*

1929   *Dido, Queen of Hearts,* for Virgil Bimillenium.

1931   *The Sophisticates.*

1932   *Adventures of a Novelist.*

1933   "Chains of the Past," chapter VI of *The Woman Accused.*

1934   *The Foghorn.*

1935   "Wanted: Imagination," *What Is a Book? Thoughts About Writing.* Received Honorary Doctor of Literature Degree, Mills College.

1936   *Golden Peacock.*

1937   Honorary Doctor of Laws Degree, University of California, Berkeley. Membership, American Society of the French Legion of Honor, Inc.

1938   *Can Women Be Gentlemen?* Elected to membership in National Institute of Arts and Letters.

1940   Named first of California's most distinguished women at San Francisco Exposition. *The House of Lee.*

1942   *The Horn of Life.*

1945   *Golden Gate Country.*

1946   *My San Francisco, A Wayward Biography.*

1948   Died June 15.

CHAPTER 1

Gertrude Atherton: Adventurer in Life and Literature

IN her autobiography, *Adventures of a Novelist* (1932)—written after forty-five years of what eventually became a sixty-year career as a novelist—Gertrude Atherton reveals that an aristocratic self-esteem, a pleasure in reading, a fascination for imagining stories, a conflict between love and independence, a concern for the poor, and a yearning to know the whole world had all characterized her childhood and young womanhood. These same elements clearly dominated her life and work.[1]

Her relatives—her ancestors, Mrs. Atherton would say—mostly Northern businessmen and a Southern belle who moved to California in the 1850s, bequeathed to her a mixture of personality traits and social attitudes that ruled her life and permeated her fiction. Born in San Francisco on October 30, 1857, she was the daughter of Gertrude Franklin, who was raised on a Louisiana plantation, and of Thomas Ludovich Horn, a businessman from Stonington, Connecticut, who achieved success in business in San Francisco. Stephen Franklin, the novelist's grandfather and a lineal descendant of Benjamin Franklin, exerted great influence on young Gertrude's intellectual development. When his business failed in Louisiana, he moved his family to San Francisco, where, though he edited the first newspaper of California and served as secretary of the Bank of California in the 1860s, his financial situation became such that he advised his daughter to marry the wealthy Horn for her future security. Franklin's character and his pioneering ownership of land in California, however, made him an aristocrat in his granddaughter's eyes. Although she rejected the harshness of his gloomy Presbyterian belief in predestination, she inherited much of his strength of personality and ambition and his scholarly interest in literature and history. In *Patience Sparhawk and Her Times* (1897), her first significant novel, the author must have imitated her grandfather in her characterization of Mr. Foord, the kindly old gentleman who encourages the young Patience to develop her mind by reading in his library in order to compensate for her isolation and poverty on a ranch.

Because of her mother's upbringing as a Southern belle, Gertrude Atherton believed that she belonged to the Southern aristocracy that was perpetuated in San Francisco in the 1850s and 1860s. However, her mother's learned supineness and her father's alcoholism and immersion in business produced a stormy marriage and a divorce. The novelist felt that she had been born of a union of antipathetic personalities and traditions and that her parents' problems were the cause of her eternal conflict between self-assertion and ladylike aristocratic manners. The invalid mother, the alcoholic father who committed suicide, and their shy daughter, Lee Tarleton, in *American Wives and English Husbands* (1898) reflect the circumstances of the real conflict in Mrs. Atherton's early life, and the fate of the women in this novel forecasts the author's lifelong interest in portraying a woman evolving out of the traditions of the past.

I   *An Undisciplined Youth and an Unfulfilled Womanhood*

Gertrude Atherton acknowledged that she was a "spoiled brat," neglected by her parents, and that her memories of San Francisco during her first score of years consisted of boredom and restless yearning to escape the "hole"of California. She did enjoy long walks and listening to the Irish songs of her nurse, Rose Stoddard. To Rose, she was indebted for warm affection and for learning the pleasure of the outdoors, which for the novelist and for many of her heroines became a place for healthy exercise and meditation.

Her parents' divorce and her mother's social ostracism when the novelist was three years of age and her stepfather's abrupt departure from San Francisco because of forgery contributed to the young Gertrude's erratic life in boardinghouses in San Francisco and on an isolated ranch. She discovered and enjoyed competition for grades with girls in private schools in the San Francisco area. At her grandfather's insistence, she learned to enjoy reading, and she began to write stories for herself and her friends. At seventeen, she attended a school in Lexington, Kentucky, where she lived with her aunt and cousins in a Southern social atmosphere and learned the pleasures of Southern flirtation and chivalry.

Summoned back in 1875 because of the failure of the Bank of California, and faced with the subsequent loss of her opportunity for a debut into San Francisco society, Gertrude Atherton rebelled against her diminished social destiny. She laid much of the blame on her mother's passivity, and she eloped with one of her mother's suitors. He was George Bowen Atherton, son of Dominga de Goñi of Valparaiso and of Dean Faxon Atherton, a native of Massachusetts, who had made a fortune in trading in Chile and California and who as a landowner was one of the first aristocrats in the Bay area. Though thwarted in her desire to read by her husband and by her Spanish mother-in-law—the latter insisting a woman's whole duty was to be a good wife, mother, and housekeeper—Mrs. Atherton nonetheless received from her and the large Atherton family the maternal attention and family stability that she had missed in her own childhood. In her autobiography, she wrote that children who have little companionship with their elders develop less character (p. 426). Despite her alleged lack of maternal instinct and of domestic virtue, Mrs. Atherton cooperated with her husband's several attempts to make a living and bore two children, who were cared for primarily by wet nurses and their grandmothers.

Incompatible with her husband because of their lack of common interests and sometimes isolated on ranches that George ineptly managed, Gertrude Atherton began to arrange outlets for her restless energy. She wrote anonymously for the *Argonaut*, a new magazine in California, and in the early 1880s persuaded her husband to establish a house in San Francisco where she could have a literary salon; out of it grew the later well-known Fortnightly Club. In the *Argonaut* in 1883 and under a pseudonym, "Asmodeus," she published the first narrative in her career-long story-chronicle of California, "The Randolphs of Redwoods." When the author and the resemblance of this narrative to an alleged actual event in the life of a prominent San Francisco family were linked, Mrs. Atherton gained the hostility of many in the San Francisco social set, and though she enjoyed the notoriety, she was again isolated from the society that she desired.[2] Nonetheless, she continued to write, and on the sudden death of her husband at sea in 1887, her restless energy and unfocused aspiration were directed in a disciplined and consistent effort to develop as a writer in New York and London.

II   Residences and Travel: "Studying the World"

The shifting of her residence from town to ranch to city in California and later to the cities of the East and of Europe, and the many relationships with different types of people developed what Mrs. Atherton knew of environmental influence and what use she would make of people and places in her fiction. Frequently she claimed her varied experiences in "studying the world" taught her to see human nature as it is, and as a writer to remain detached as she narrated the peaks and chasms of human experience.[3]

Her youth in San Francisco coincided with the turbulent growth of California and San Francisco from the Arcadian Spanish-Mexican era to one influenced by gold, Yankee businessmen, and displaced aristocratic Southern families. She observed the behavior of different classes of people in various places: the festivities of the señoras, the caballeros, and las favoritas of the "splendid idle forties"; the millionaires from the South and the North with homes on Rincon Hill and in the "country" at Menlo Park and Burlingame; the relentless drive of the invading businessmen; the monotonous routine of neighbors' visits, veranda conversations, and eight-course meals in the country; the dull existences behind the blind-drawn windows of middle-class homes and boardinghouses in San Francisco; the poor living areas of the Spanish, the Japanese, and Chinese immigrants. Throughout her story-chronicle of California, depicted from 1800 to 1938, Mrs. Atherton created types of characters from the lower, middle and aristocratic classes; she endowed them with certain inherited traits and placed them in circumstances that lifted them out of their ordinary fates. Her fictional characters, especially her independent, intellectual California women, acted out the struggle between the conditions of a place—a sunny environment conducive to complacency—and their heritage of social attitudes. The pursuit of happiness—a life purpose whether in California or anywhere else in the United States, in England, or in Europe—became one of her major motifs. Among the fifteen novels, written between 1892 and 1942, that portray this California heroine, *The Californians*, in which both the heroine and California undergo initiation, stands out as one of her best.

Mrs. Atherton's departure from California in 1888 seemed necessary to her development as a writer. She appeared to thrive on hotel and apartment living, for she established a residence wherever she needed to gain a story idea or to write or to sell a book. From 1888 to 1931, when she returned to San Francisco to live, she alternated her residences between New York and London, between the Continent (especially in Munich) and London, and between New York and California.[4] Unlike fellow expatriate Henry James, she steadily nurtured her American roots by returning to the United States in alternate years. Her pattern of writing a book consisted of imagining a motif for a story, researching it in libraries or on the site of the motif, and then residing in a place entirely different from the fictional setting so that her imagination would not be distracted by the local reality (p. 271). She wrote *The Californians* in rural England, and her political romance of Washington at the turn of the century, *Senator North* (1900), came to life in Bruges, Belgium.

To New York, London, and Munich, the aristocratic Gertrude Atherton carried letters of introduction, and immediately was entertained by personalities prominent in social, literary, political, and publishing circles. Her association with them frequently aided her literary imagination, sharpened her historical insight, and developed her self-confidence in matters both literary and critical. Among many others, she met Thomas Hardy, Henry James, and James Whistler, and achieved her first literary acclaim in London before critics in New York gave her serious attention.

In the 1890s, British magazines readily accepted her short stories of early California as well as those with supernatural themes. And her realistic-romantic rendition of aspiring California women and European-American marriages pleased British readers, eager to have her country interpreted for them. In *The Aristocrats* (1901), an epistolary novel published anonymously, Mrs. Atherton wittily exposed the pretensions of some American literary and fashionable types from the point of view of an intelligent, young English noblewoman. The American reviewers' praise of this novel before her authorship was known amused Mrs. Atherton even as she acknowledged that she had tactlessly alienated a few critics (pp. 339 - 40).

In New York City during World War I, Gertrude Atherton relied on her upper-class social contacts to organize the raising of funds for military hospitals, which she later visited in France. Increasingly sensitive to popular middle-class notions, she exchanged opinions on feminism, both French and American, on writing fiction, and on the Germans in articles and letters in New York newspapers. These years and those following the war marked her shift of attention from society and literature, as they usually are conceived, toward a concern with the ideas, feelings, and reactions of a popular reading audience. Her writing of mystery stories, her script-writing for Samuel Goldwyn in Hollywood in 1921, and her fiction featuring popularly under-stood Freudian notions as in *The Crystal Cup* (1925) all reflected the growing democratic scope of her interests and her associa-tions in her varied places of residence. *Black Oxen* (1923), depicting New York in the Roaring Twenties, became a best-seller, and its movie version in 1924 made a star of Corinne Griffith.

Several times curiosity drove Gertrude Atherton to the adventure of travel for original research. Her admiration of Alexander Hamilton led her to dig into church and registry records in the Virgin Islands and Denmark in order to attempt to prove the legitimacy of Hamilton's birth and to persuade the readers of her biographical novel, *The Conqueror* (1902), that Hamilton contributed significantly to his adopted country. Her invention of such a biography, using the methods of fiction in the genre so that she could be a "correct historian" of her own times while making the past live again for her readers, should earn for Mrs. Atherton a more significant place in American literature; one critic has suggested that *The Conqueror* as biographical fiction antedates what later was known as the "Maurois school."[5]

Mrs. Atherton used this form again to prove that the greatest love story of the ages—that of Aspasia and Pericles—was not diminished by her research in Athens that uncovered Aspasia's role, not as a *hetaera* but as a woman accepting the "respecta-ble"role of a morganatic wife (p. 568). Two weeks in Greece in 1925 and several months spent in the intellectual adventure of reading two hundred books on the Golden Age of Athens produced two biographical novels. One, *The Immortal Marriage* (1927), recreated the marriage of Aspasia and Pericles, and the other, *The Jealous Gods* (1928), related the procession of Alcibiades to power in Athens. Though sales of these two books were light, Greek scholars approved them and placed them on college library shelves (p. 577).

Having returned to permanent residence in San Francisco in 1931, Gertrude Atherton wrote her autobiography to sum up her "adventures" as a novelist in many places. In view of the loss of the personal papers dealing with the first fifty years of her life in the San Francisco earthquake and fire of 1906 and in view of her age, the autobiography—more a memoir than an intimate account of her life—is a remarkable feat of memory and a witty, candid, and detached description of herself and of the thousands of friends and acquaintances known in three quarters of a century. In her native state, which three decades before she had considered a "hole," Mrs. Atherton continued to write fiction and nonfiction primarily concerned with San Francisco and its environs, and she took a social, civic, and literary position in her birthplace that earned for her in 1940 the honor of being the first to be named California's most distinguished woman. Her last two novels, *The House of Lee* (1940) and *The Horn of Life* (1942), relate how near to the goal of their quests for identity were her California woman and her city, San Francisco.

III   *Personal and Professional Friendships and Associations*

Gertrude Atherton's unsettled childhood and youth and the large Atherton family introduced her to a variety of relationships. Yet the author appeared to struggle against the need for love and to foster a desire to be free of love's demands. She once remarked that she grew up with the idea that marriage consisted of bickering and quarrels, and because her own youthful marriage apparently did not fill a need, she doubted then and for the rest of her life that she had ever been in love. It is indicative of her paradoxical view of reality that she recognized the conflict between art and marriage and between self-identity and social duty, and that this basic conflict, which she envisioned as a life force and located, in part, in the relationship between man and woman, would be a major motif in her fiction.

Gertrude Atherton attracted as close friends women who like

herself aspired to active lives of their own. Sybil Sanderson, a friend of her youth and daughter of a judge in San Francisco, fulfilled her ambition to become an opera star. In Paris in 1889, Mrs. Atherton attended Sanderson's debut in *Esclarmonde*, written for her by Massenet (pp. 112, 159). Mrs. Atherton's letters to Minnie Maddern Fiske, the well-known actress for whom she attempted to write a play with a feminist character in 1910 - 1911, reveal the stimulation and frustration of friendship between two self-centered professional people.[6] She also developed mutually rewarding associations with women who wrote both fiction and journalism for periodicals and newspapers. Among these were Elizabeth Jordan of the *New York World*, a writer of mystery stories; Honoré Willsie, editor of the *Delineator*; Isabel Paterson, novelist and book reviewer of the *New York Herald Tribune*; and Hildegarde Hawthorne, granddaughter of Nathaniel Hawthorne, author, and writer for the *New York Times*. Through these friends, Mrs. Atherton was able to secure reviews of her books and assistance in the publication of her articles on issues that concerned her. In several of her novels, women characters as journalists or writers of fiction—Patience Sparhawk in *Patience Sparhawk and Her Times* and Gora Dwight in *The Sisters-in-Law* and *Black Oxen*— figure importantly in the plots

Mrs. Atherton did not limit her personal and professional friendships to women. Though she never remarried because a persistent voice in her subconscious warned her not to (p. 173), she continued to develop a variety of friendships with men, and perhaps loved a few of them. In her autobiograhy, she wrote that an absorbing interest in a new man afforded mental stimulation which inspired a book, but that as soon as the book was ready to be born, the man ceased to interest her and was tactfully or abruptly discarded (p. 107). Although this autobiographical wit could merely reflect a woman's version of the male aphorism of taking or leaving love, Mrs. Atherton acknowledged her doubt about ever having been in love. Among her deep friendships were those with such personalities as James Duval Phelan, mayor of San Francisco and a United States Senator (pp. 414 - 15); writer-critics such as Gelett Burgess, Ambrose Bierce, and Hilaire Belloc; Charles Hanson Towne, writer and actor; Upton Sinclair, novelist and Socialist; and Carl Van Vechten, novelist, who insisted that she write her autobiography (p. 559). She was accepted in the academic and social communities of Columbia University, Stanford University, and the University of California, Berkeley, and gained from academic friendships some guidance for the background of the four novels dealing with classical times. She received from Mills College an Honorary Doctor of Literature degree in 1935 and from the Universty of California, Berkeley, an Honorary Doctor of Laws degree in 1937. She was elected to membership in the National Institute of Arts and Letters in 1938.

The pages of her unpublished letters and her autobiography testify to the importance of her acquaintances among editors, publishers, and critics. Many of these correspondents she valued as personal friends, but she also sought their support in gaining publication, especially of her early work, and recognition that she believed her books deserved. The struggles of an unknown writer from California to be published in the East at the turn of the century are revealed in Mrs. Atherton's letters from 1888 to 1898 to Joseph M. Stoddart, editor of *Lippincott's Magazine*,[7] which in 1892 published *The Doomswoman*, the old California story with which the novelist acknowledged her real writing career began. The problems of a woman as a novelist earning a living are disclosed in letters to publishers John Lane and John Murray of London and to the avant-garde Horace Liveright of New York, and to such of her editors as John Williams of D. Appleton - Century and T. R. Smith of Liveright. Her good friend Joseph Henry Jackson, critic and columnist of the *San Francisco Chronicle*, offered during her lifetime the only separate review of all of her work up to her 1940 novel, *The House of Lee*. Her correspondence with these editors and writers also indicates some of the currents and influences impinging on her during her sixty-year career.

Because of her frequent residence in London and elsewhere over the years, Gertrude Atherton knew and admired many writers, British and American (particularly Californian). Many times in the pages of British and American publications, she argued both sides of the question of the superiority of English or American fiction.[8] During her sojourns in London, she met H. G. Wells, John Galsworthy, W. Somerset Maugham, and other major and minor writers. She did not meet Arnold Bennett, whose *The Old Wives' Tale* she admired. Her autobiography contains many anecdotes about famous literary and social personages of

London. One afternoon, Mrs. Atherton called on Lady Colin
Campbell, a London hostess and critic, who, seductively dressed,
appeared to be expecting a man to call. To Mrs. Atherton's
surprise, the man was Henry James (pp. 284 - 85). A scene
reflecting the tensions of this encounter was recreated in her
novel *Ancestors* (1907).

In the early 1880s, Mrs. Atherton admired William Dean
Howells and caught the "Henry James craze" in California, even
though she believed that James's manner was "too aristocratic,
too lofty, too detached," to command as large a following as that
of middle-class Howells (p. 107). Nevertheless, she wrote several
novels with a Jamesian European-American theme. James
reviewed two of these novels—*His Fortunate Grace* (1897) and
American Wives and English Husbands (1898). In both he found
elements "sharply satiric" of the attitudes that the English and
the Americans held toward each other, and he expressed
puzzlement concerning her intention in depicting the American-
English "relation of the sexes."[9] James appeared not to com-
prehend the point of view of Mrs. Atherton's willful American
heroines.

The California author was usually overwhelmed by James's
kind of articulateness when on three social occasions she met him
in London, and it took Edmund Gosse's advice to her to read
James's last novels before she came to appreciate his "genius."
One might speculate that Mrs. Atherton's heroine in *The
Californians* (1898), who yearns to write in the manner of James
but who ultimately admits that she cannot master words, speaks
for her creator. Then, in 1905, during James's return to America
after a twenty-year absence, Gertrude Atherton in an article in
the *Argonaut* praised the masterful psychology in his fiction.[10]
She wrote a long short story, "The Bell in the Fog," in which
James is the hero, though alienated from his American heritage;
she dedicated the volume of short stories in which the story
appeared in 1905 to "Henry James the Master." The short story
appears to comment on the negative effect on James's writing of
his long exile from America;[11] and although Mrs. Atherton also
exiled herself from her country, for different reasons, she could
point to the fact that in alternate years she returned to New York
or to California and kept in touch with American writers, even
California ones such as George Sterling, Mary Austin, Ina

Coolbrith, Charles Caldwell Dobie, and Charles and Kathleen Norris.

Gertrude Atherton appeared to know well none of the American women novelists of her time. Ellen Glasgow and Mary Austin attended her wartime salon in New York, and she met and corresponded with Gertrude Stein; apparently she never met Willa Cather or Edith Wharton, the latter her alleged rival as a novelist of New York.[12] In the ongoing debate over the superiority of English or American fiction, Ellen Glasgow asserted in 1916 that contemporary English novels were superior to American ones because the "evasive idealism" of American readers and writers was reflected in literature and in every phase of American life. Mrs. Atherton agreed with Glasgow's description of American readers, but disagreed with her assertion of better English fiction by claiming that English readers widely accepted the romantic stories of Gene Stratton Porter and Marie Corelli.[13] In 1932, Mrs. Atherton served on the committee of the *Prix Fémina Americain* that selected Willa Cather's *Shadows on the Rocks* (1931) as one of three winners. In several articles in periodicals, Mrs. Artherton referred to women novelists of England, but accounts of friendship with her contemporaries, Mrs. Humphrey Ward, May Sinclair, or others, do not exist.

IV   *The Reading of an Adventurer: "Feeding a Serious Turn of Mind"*

Gertrude Atherton read widely and purposefully throughout her life. Her earliest preference for *Little Women, Jane Eyre,* Ouida's romances, and Oliver Optic stories was followed by her grandfather's attempt to educate her, against her fourteen-year-old will, to a taste for serious reading, a taste for which she later admitted being forever grateful (p. 29). Although not formally educated, Mrs. Atherton later used the early discipline of reading when she investigated a narrative idea with a scholar's methods and perseverance in order to create authentic milieu and characterizations in her fiction. Critics commented frequently on her skill as a panoramist. Perhaps her meager formal education provided less constraint on the powers of observation, perception, and imagination of her "untutored and wholly

feminine mind" (p. 244). However, it might also explain what
some critics have called the superficial rendition of unassimi-
lated ideas and the uneven tone in her novels. Her written
comments on her lifelong reading are cryptic and scattered in
occasional interviews and published articles, and more extensive
study of them is needed in order to draw an adequate picture of
the relationship between her reading and her fiction.

Early in her childhood and marriage, Mrs. Atherton's reading
frequently compensated for emotional turmoil. Her grandfather's insistence that she read aloud to him from the historical
and literary classics in his fine library probably developed the
author's appreciation of the sounds and rhythms of language as
well as of the thoughts and ideas of great minds of the past.
Exposure to the past nurtured her own ambition to be a "correct
historian" of her times in order to extend her readers' knowledge
of the larger world by showing the connection between the past
and their own times.[14]

From Washington Irving's *The Conquest of Granada*, Thiers's
History of the French Revolution, and Hume's *History of Great
Britain*, her grandfather graduated her to the poetry, not of her
early favorites Bryant and Longfellow, but of Chaucer,
Shakespeare, Shelley, and Byron, the last poet being credited
with awakening the feminine consciousness of Mrs. Atherton's
first significant heroine, Patience Sparhawk. Determined to be
well read to compensate for her social isolation, she plowed
through Herodotus, Thucydides, and Xenophon, Voltaire's
Philosophical Dictionary, Goldsmith's *Citizen of the World*,
Fiske's *Outlines of Cosmic Philosophy*, and a whole set of Walter
Scott's romances (pp. 79, 89, 101).

Reflecting this learned pleasure in serious reading, Gertrude
Atherton purchased, with the first check earned by a published
story, not novels but the

collected speeches of Fox, Burke, Pitt, and Daniel Webster;
Gladstone's *Gleanings of Past Years* (duller than Hume); Emerson's
Essays; Macaulay's *Essays* and *History of England*; Kinglake's *History
of the Crimean War* and *Eōthen; Vathek;* Herbert Spencer's *First
Principles* and his Essay on Style; Pepys' and Evelyn's *Diaries*; Taine's
History of English Literature; Richard Grant White's *Words and Their
Uses; the Moonstone,* and several volumes of Daudet. (p.96)

From Taine she derived her characterization of fictional types,
and from Spencer she gained her notion of an individual style for

each of her books and the idea of a universal Creative Force that interacted with imaginative and original minds of the past and present.[15] The importance that Gertrude Atherton attached to serious reading is reflected in the names of the books that her favored characters display in their libraries.

Mrs. Atherton's early desire to become an author was nurtured by her continuous reading of fiction, popular and classic, Romantic and Realistic, American, English, and European. This eclecticism helped her to discover her audience—the "bourgeois," i.e. middle-class, audience whose provincial world she hoped to enlarge. She read, and sometimes praised, the work of such popular romancers as Edgar Saltus, Helen Hunt Jackson, Robert Chambers, Robert Hichens, Winston Churchill, Paul Leicester Ford, and Mary Johnston.[16] Her interest in these writers offset her antipathy to the thin anemic literature of the Realists, especially of William Dean Howells. She claimed that each year she reread the Greek tragedies, and her reading of Plato resulted in her utilizing as a theme in several novels the notion of two souls seeking union. Mark Twain and Howells, she declared, had the greatest influence on American writers, and she followed Howells's advice in his *Harper's* columns to read Spanish and Russian novelists. As a part of her reaction against Howells, she complained of the dreary Gorki and the lack of architecture in Tolstoi's *Anna Karenina*, and when it was fashionable to criticize bolshevism, she labeled Russia as "that criminal among nations."[17]

As a young girl, Gertrude Atherton read *Jane Eyre* six times and considered it "a pioneer book, a gesture of defiance at the traditions of the era." However, after living for a short time in Haworth, the village of the Brontës, while she wrote *A Daughter of the Vine*, she regarded *Jane Eyre* as an "old-fashioned melodrama" and transferred her esteem to Emily Brontë as "the most interesting and tragic figure in all literature" (pp. 237, 242). Several of Walter Pater's ideas attracted Mrs. Atherton's attention. His use of paganism, with its emphasis upon the development of an ideal aesthetic temperament and his idea of the unattainable lover, became an element that she incorporated in her characterizations of a new and modern Helen. She also appeared to be well read in and influenced by the French novels that were translated for American readers at the turn of the century. To avoid further controversy with her publishers and reviewers in regard to her sensational themes, Mrs. Atherton allowed several characters to decry the eroticism of French novels. She once complained, however, that the preference of readers in San Francisco for the neatly resolved plots of Maupassant indicated their unawareness of the complex world. With the practicality of one who wrote for a living, Gertrude Atherton frequently spoke out on literary trends and social issues. In an article in 1910, her catalogue of the American novels read in England showed the range of her reading and her knowledge of the sales of American writers. The list included the popular—Mrs. Wiggin and Amélie Rives; the obscure—Elizabeth Jordan; the easily recognized—Frank Norris, Edith Wharton, Owen Wister; the Californians—Ambrose Bierce, Bret Harte, Mary Austin, and Jack London.[18] In 1922, concerned about the effect of immigration from southern Europe and from the Orient, she called on young writers—Sinclair Lewis, John Dos Passos, Charles Norris, and others—to write about the cause of the progress of humanity, which she attributed mainly to the Anglo-Saxon race rather than to class.[19]

Mrs. Atherton gradually extended her reading and purchases of books on European history and philosophy, perhaps representative of an aristocratic viewpoint, to American historians and writers on democratic and social issues. Henry George's ideas on the problem of the poor and the rich motivate the hero of *Los Cerritos* (1890) to resolve a squatter's strike in the Central Valley of California. Later she read books on socialism, involved a few of her characters in university study of the issue in *The Sisters-in-Law* (1921) and in *The House of Lee* (1940), and feuded with Upton Sinclair on the implications of socialism. From *Los Cerritos* to her last novel in 1942, Mrs. Atherton traced the evolution, or progress, of the human race from the milieu of the *noblesse oblige* of the aristocratic few to the widening choices of life purpose by individuals exposed to the tenets of capitalism, socialism, bolshevism, and democracy. In the prefaces and afterwords to her biographical and historical novels and her history and geographies of California, she catalogued the extent of her reading in the preparation of authentic backgrounds.

In her novels, Mrs. Atherton displays the influence of her reading of political economy, social philosophy, and history less in a fictional report on the progress of Western institutions than in her thematic emphasis on the effect of these institutions and the customs associated with them on the individual, especially on women. The pursuit of happiness—the individual's questioning of or questing for a purpose in life within the boundary of social institutions—serves as her major and basic fictional motif. Her characters react to the varied forces that either constrain them or free them to develop themselves fully and happily. Her historical women characters, such as Aspasia and Dido, and her imagined contemporary women, especially her California women, demonstrate her concept of "un-ordinary" women, who attempt to relate their inner natures to their outer circumstances. Such models as Madame de Staël, Madame Récamier, Ninon de l'Enclos, and many contemporary women lead her to claim that the highest intelligences are anarchic and critical of the commonplace, conventional expectations of women in the Western world. As a social historian, Mrs. Atherton observed the American divorce rate rising since the late 1860s, the increasing number of working women, the strains on the family in an industrial age, and the ennui that afflicts the idle person. As a result, she employed fictional methods to explore women's choices of a life purpose proffered by these social and economic changes. Ultimately, in her hands, the historical and the typical romance that was popular with the large middle-class women's audience became less a heroic and romantic adventure and more a "psychological drama," an adventure of a woman finding her goal in living.[20] At the time of her death in 1948 at the age of ninety, Gertrude Atherton was still adventuring herself—writing a novel about quicksilver mining in California.

CHAPTER 2

The Art and Craft of an Original, Imaginative Writer

G ERTRUDE Atherton was frequently asked why and how she wrote and what she thought of writers and literature. Over the years, she expressed her thoughts on writing and literature in articles in magazines and newspapers, or in response to questions posed by interviewers. However, she never collected these occasional expressions into a cohesive statement about the original, imaginative writer she was calling for in American literature. In her first novels as well as in articles, interviews, and letters published in New York, San Francisco, and London, she discoursed often but cryptically on the art of fiction and the craft of writing. Her autobiography of 1932 deals with people and events, seldom with literary matters.

Her first and rambling effort to express her literary creed appeared in 1904 in the *North American Review* and is entitled "Why Is American Literature Bourgeois?" Thirty years later she discussed the question again in "Wanted: Imagination" (1935).[1] In the first essay, she offers observations about her creed of originality and imagination. She was reacting against the middle-class (bourgeois) conformity that suppressed individual aspiration, against what she called the thin, anemic Realistic writing that obscured for readers the peaks and chasms of human existence and the knowledge of the great world beyond their provincial lives, and against the formulaic magazine style that denied publication to the innovative writer.[2] With her perception of the conflict between writer and publisher and with her reaction against social and literary attitudes, Mrs. Atherton's creed became a strategy for interaction between herself and her audience—which for her included critics, reviewers, and her own set of readers—and between herself and her books. She staked her literary reputation on her storytelling originality and imagination rather than on a basic aesthetic theory or a literary school. An examination of her occasional writings suggests that her creed changed very little in sixty years, and provides the materials needed to evaluate her literary achievement and her contribution to American literature.

In the late 1880s, when Mrs. Atherton began to indulge in coherent dreams of a literary career and of making a living by writing, she had attempted no formal study of literature or of literary conditions—the interaction of writer, publisher, reader, and critic with a book. She expected a Californian chivalry to be shown toward her by publishers and editors. Although disappointed by editors' rejections and by the reviewers' scorn of the unusual themes and characters of her first two novels, *What Dreams May Come* (1888) and *Hermia Suydam* (1889), Mrs. Atherton pragmatically persisted in writing in her own original and imaginative way in order to keep her fiction noticed.

Once she gained the usually favorable attention of London reviewers and readers, she utilized this acclaim as a wedge to get publication and approval of her books in America. In controversy she discovered a strategy for attracting the attention of reviewers and for earning a living as a writer. She accurately assessed the value of her work in the literary marketplace. She learned to negotiate effective contracts with her publishers, sometimes by pitting one against another, by developing a personality ready to face conflict, and by forming friendships with editors, owners of publishing houses, and reviewers who would provide favorable reception of her books.

Furthermore, although she claimed to be aloof, serving "art as the most jealous of all mistresses," Mrs. Atherton studied the responses of readers and reviewers in order to identify the audience for her particular fictional concerns. Desirous of escaping her experience of isolation, monotony, and ennui— conditions she associated with the traditional role for a woman— she imagined that women as major readers of romances and novels shared her attitude, and that they should have their knowledge of the great world extended and their spirits uplifted, even while being entertained. Believing that novelists are the best current historians of the great world,[3] she became a conscious craftsman of the novel and carefully selected for fiction, material that had both contemporaneity—the world as

she saw it[4]—and romantic elements appealing to her audience.
She reasoned that writers had no right to ask people to buy their
books if they could not relay to readers, without preaching,
something they did not know before.[5] She believed that
literature did not and must not tell readers how they should
believe and live their lives. Hence her literary creed, perceived
wholly, appears to be a pragmatic one that unites writer, book,
and reader in an instructive and mutually affective artistic
relationship.

I   The Original, Imaginative Writer:
"Head and Shoulders above the Mass"

Gertrude Atherton's concern for the original, imaginative
writer was based, in part, on what she called the failure of the
kind of originality of Bret Harte and Mark Twain to influence
subsequent American writers and on her vision of a literary
expression of the "genius of the American race." In her essay,
"Why Is American Literature Bourgeois?" (1904), she contrasted Harte's and Twain's peculiarly American literature with
the prevailing New England Realism. The New England
influence on literature, she insisted, produced a literature that
was "the most timid, the most anaemic, the most lacking in
individualities, the most bourgeois, that any country has ever
known." By "bourgeois" she meant middle class, and she
complained that current writers avoided dealing with the
"boldness and dynamic energy that had made the progress of the
United States phenomenal in the history of the nations." For this
anemia, she blamed not only William Dean Howells, whose
realism she branded as "littleism" and as a blight on American
literature, but also the established writers of the formulaic
magazine school, which smothered the genius of new writers like
a "leech at the throat of originality."[6]

Mrs. Atherton carried her complaint into her first novels. Two
major characters in *What Dreams May Come* (1888), a novel of
reincarnation, decry the thinness of characterization by the
"chief expounders [presumably Howells and Henry James] of
the American girl at home and abroad," and the rebellious
heroine in *Hermia Suydam* (1889) has her manuscript rejected
by an editor who thinks it too highly emotional for a family
magazine which a father might want his daughter to read.[7]

In "Illustrious Seconds" in the *North American Review,* Mrs. Atherton reacted to unfavorable American reviews of these novels by attempting to define the original, imaginative writer. In arguing against the critics' classifying a new, praiseworthy writer as "second" to an already-established author, Mrs. Atherton explained her idea of an original, imaginative one:

The literature of one generation, even of one decade, is the natural result of the literature immediately preceding it; evolution is inexorable. But upon this force of heredity operate the great and complex forces of the times, and the man who is thrust head and shoulders above the mass, as the target of his generation and a landmark for posterity, is he in whom both forces have met and been ignited by the divine spark that shot in his unborn brain, whence no man can tell.[8]

In view of this environmentally affected inborn gift and of the writer's purpose to add to the knowledge of mankind, the writer, Gertrude Atherton maintained, is obliged "to study unceasingly the great map of life," to divorce himself from all that is snug, comfortable, and orthodox, and to descend to the "vast underworld where the greatest writers have found their inspirations."[9] This charge to the original, imaginative writer and the defiance of social and literary conventions by her heroines mirror Mrs. Atherton's reaction to the Realists' presentation of the small, unimaginative contents of middle-class life.

The California novelist admired both Sainte-Beuve, to whom criticism was a moral exploration through literature but without dogmatism, and Hippolyte Taine, whose tripartite view of literary criticism offered a theory rather than a judgment of literature and founded a psychology of a people. Sainte-Beuve and Taine set her direction as an original, imaginative writer. Hence she told stories that explored the psychology of the peaks and valleys of her characters' lives, not morally to instruct but to entertain and to extend the worldly knowledge of her readers.

How was a writer to avoid the timidity and conformity of Howells and the magazine writers? Gertrude Atherton urged writers to shun identification with a school and the faddism which yields to the habits or whims of the reader. She contrasted Edith Wharton's fiction, which she described as conforming to the precepts of the Realists, with that of Henry James, who symbolized the great writer with knowledge of the wider world who broke loose from literary and social tradition and wrote in his own manner.[10] Furthermore, she contrasted such "born creators" as Harte and Mary E. Wilkins with writers who possess a "manufactured set of mind."[11] She attributed to the born writer instinct, imagination, and lifelikeness, all characteristics that would reflect the complexity of human experience and produce illusion and startling effect. The attributes of the manufactured writer, on the other hand, were form, technique, artifice, and mere observation of people, all creating in literature the static and safe effect on the reader that, she thought, was desired by the literary establishment. Attempting to draw a fine line between the two types of writer, Mrs. Atherton described a manufactured writer as creating an effect like that of a Chinese painting, flat against the canvas, whereas the born writer achieved a third dimension—like a vital moss covering a stone—by breathing life and the unexpected complexities of life into the characters.

Writing on imagination again in 1935, Mrs. Atherton maintained her contrast of writers in terms of the genius and the craftsman; one type possessed a magic like that of Henry James and Arnold Bennett, glorifying facts by imagination and sustaining the novel's movement; the other possessed a satisfactory craftsmanship, fictionized facts, and a purposeful theme.[12] Her identification of herself with the born genius is implied in both essays.

These generalizations concerning the original, imaginative writer can be illustrated with one of Mrs. Atherton's best and most well-received novels, *The Conqueror, Being the True and Romantic Story of Alexander Hamilton* (1902). After research into Hamilton's early years in the West Indies and in Denmark and after reading seven biographies of him, she applied the methods of fiction to biographical fact and produced a "true and romantic story" of this historical figure whom she thoroughly admired. In effect, she invented the biographical novel. And in her concept of herself as a correct historian of her age, she recreated the life of Hamilton in relief against his own times and environment, and through her narrator's comments, she linked the actions and the attitudes of Hamilton's lifetime to their effects in her own. These creative efforts resulted in her narrating the heretofore unknown story of Hamilton's parents' unwed romance; in elaborating details of his domestic and social life, his relations with his paramours, and his filial devotion to

George Washington; and in her characterizing Hamilton as equal, if not superior, to James Madison and Thomas Jefferson in his contribution to the development of the American republic. Reviewers generally praised the original form and the technique of the novel, though a few objected to her glorification of Hamilton and his amours at the expense of lesser portraits of Madison and Jefferson.

Gertrude Atherton's career spanned sixty years, during which time more women wrote seriously about themselves and about the real world as they saw it. After a score of years spent in achieving a reputation as a novelist, she could argue that certain brain cells, the creative faculty, had no sex.[13] Yet she observed that, because of middle-class values, very few women writers were original and imaginative. They did not know how to use their liberty to recognize the peaks and chasms of life, or how to regard life impersonally and as a spectacle, or how to disassociate the mind from the body (which they believed was to be deified as a symbol of beauty and youth). To Mrs. Atherton, women as writers were handicapped, "the miserable victims" of their own personalities, which had been constructed by traditional expectations of a woman's role.

The typical woman writer, she noted, knowing society's expectations and afraid to be honest about her own perceptions of a woman's existence, made her characters citizens of a kind of materialized hereafter,[14] or she shrank from presenting the real human drama at the psychological movement of revelation. This curious shrinking she noticed in the writing of British women, a withdrawal that in Mrs. Humphrey Ward's work she called the "hot water and yellow soap treatment" of life.[15] Out of her own experience, and desiring to be acknowledged by reviewers and readers as a serious artist, Mrs. Atherton advised women to develop their intellects, but she also admitted that the body— beauty and magnetism—was as valuable for the success of a woman writer as for an actress.[16] She urged women to perceive life at first hand and, in particular, to learn to write by taking jobs on newspapers, where they would lose their nonsensical and sentimental notions and learn the principles of composition. Drawing on her own experience, she imagined a newspaper job for Patience Sparhawk as a part of her initiation into knowledge of the world.

II   *The Book: "A Memoir of Contemporary Life"*
and a Correct History

Gertrude Atherton's early ambition to write stories and her
reading of history predicted that fiction would be her matter and
the novel the form it would take. Informally educated, she had to
construct her own sense of reality and her literary attitude
toward it, so that the form of her writing—whether fiction or
non-fiction—would rise instinctively from what she called her
fictional tract. Novelists seek truth and are the best current
historians, she told an interviewer,[17] and one of her intellectual
characters, Ora Stratton in *Perch of the Devil* (1914), remarks
that the best of fiction is the best expression of current history.
These comments indicate Atherton's belief that the novelist was
one part fictionist, imagining the characters and problems of
modern society, and one part social historian, recording the
values and actions of the times. The work of serious novelists,
writing current history, Mrs. Atherton regarded as valuable a
source of future reference as the efforts of the more labored
historian.[18]

Beginning to write when the Realists were reacting against the
domestic novel and the historical romance and when the
numbers of novels and of the middle-class women readers were
increasing simultaneously, Mrs. Atherton served as a catalyst for
the union of the romance and the novel. As a woman newly
awakened in a democracy,[19] she saw for herself and others
expanding opportunities for personal and social development,
and as a "correct historian" of her times she was determined to
record them in fiction. She relied on a novelist's instinct,
unmolded by literary tradition, to imagine unusual circumstances
that would develop the latent potentialities of selected types of
characters. Although she acknowledged that men and women
reacted both instinctively and rationally to circumstances, she
avoided the literary naturalistic pessimism by realistically
presenting her characters' foolish and wise thoughts and actions
without moralizing them. Following Taine and studying their
inner life, she created a psychological realism in her characterizations. Furthermore, her claim to correctness was based on
her experience of the world as it is, which she attempted to
record accurately by carrying out her theme and characterizations to their logical end.[20]

Mrs. Atherton utilized her California material to experiment with the romance and the novel as forms. Her stories of aspiring characters, interacting with their environment in California or elsewhere, loosely combined the romance and the novel. Employing the elements of romance, she could present the events and characters of California's little known and romantic past. Joining romance and the methods of the novel, she could draw aspiring and self-conflicted characters who reflected actual situations and opportunities of women from the 1890s onward and that contemporary Realistic novels, in her opinion, denied the reader. "A memoir of contemporary life in the form of fiction" is the definition of the novel provided by Mrs. Atherton's fictional novelist, Gora Dwight, in *The Sisters-in-Law*;[21] Gora, a loser in romance, writes a novel of California, whose "grim relentless logic" and "romantic realism made its tragedy more poignant." As late as 1935, Mrs. Atherton declared that a judicious blend of the Romantic and the Realistic had become for her the only type of novel that was "true to life."[22]

Gertrude Atherton believed that the writer of fiction must endow reality—the plan of life—with an inventive and imaginative expression which communicates its meaning. A theme centralizes a novel and adds to its dignity and importance, but more pertinent to her was the belief that the true novel is a living entity, created by a writer who instinctively knows the elements out of which the novel's illusion of reality comes. To her these primary elements would include the human ego, needing love, desiring freedom, reacting to circumstances that affect it and that in turn become new causes of action which would or would not fulfill the ego's basic drive for happiness. In her view, the rendering of the interaction of the brain, the will, physical needs, and environment—all affecting the ego of the character—creates the novel's illusion of reality.

Hence the novel, like life itself, she maintained, consists of "a succession of reactions" to circumstances that in turn cause new incidents "peculiar to the people portrayed." If the novel is like life, then it would have to vary in form, and "its constant sense of adventure" and the "expectancy, the apprehension . . . in the characters" would dictate that the novel could never have the perfection of form available to the expert dramatist, the short story writer composing an episode, or the romancer narrating incidents for their own sake.[23] Therefore the form and style of each of her novels reflected a plan of life peculiar to its theme and its characters.

At the core of Mrs. Atherton's view of reality is the familiar ancient conflict of nature and civilization, out of which she spun her own web of oppositions and categories of cause and effect. The primal instinct of the race to perpetuate itself versus a rational selection of a mate; energy versus ennui; race versus class or heredity vis-à-vis environment; individuality versus tradition; freedom versus security; body versus brain—all of these conflicts, in her view, had effects on people and caused them to react in ways peculiar to them. The conflicts appeared to be governed by two general laws: The Law of Circumstances, which has biological, psychological, and social aspects with which the individual has to cope in the process of discovering and pursuing a life purpose; and the Law of Compensation, which, the individual comes to understand, gives order or balance to the opposing forces affecting her or him.

To translate this plan of life into the novel, Mrs. Atherton invented themes, characters, and incidents that, to her, originally and imaginatively reflected the "bold, dynamic energy" of a young nation and its people. She created a type of independent, willful, adventuresome woman and placed her in an idyllic, young state; both the woman and the state, symbolizing human aspiration and egotistic illusion, earned the epithet of "fool's paradise." The circumstances of early and modern California, with its arcadian environment, its geographical isolation, and its historic amalgam of old-world aristocratic customs, New England aggressiveness and morality, and Southern manners composed one of Mrs. Atherton's settings; in it the young nation attempted to work out its internal conflicts and to discover its direction and destiny. The woman, her ego circumscribed by traditional religious belief, social custom, and lack of self-knowledge, was the focus of the contradictions of Circumstances and the instrument of Compensation as well as a means of portraying unchanging human nature in an increasingly complex civilization. The California woman was Mrs. Atherton's prototype of an evolving "Woman of Tomorrow,"[24] and as she also narrated the adventures and self-conflicts of this type in America's Midwest, in New York, England, and Munich, she seemed to suggest that the American woman might in turn cause a change in Western civilization.

Affinity—the attraction between man and woman that under-
lies civilization and insures the future of the race—is Mrs.
Atherton's basic term for the expression of this reality of
conflicts and for her characterization of the California woman.
Like "life-force," "affinity" at the turn of the century was a
much-used word; it popularly denoted romantic love that ended
in early marriage or it alluded to a Neoplatonic idea that a soul
seeks unity in another soul.[25] Mrs. Atherton frequently had her
heroine fantasize a soul-mate—a conventional Romantic
notion—but one which she employed to characterize an anti-
Romantic, self-aggrandizing woman, one who might stimulate
the imaginations of her middle-class readers more than the
sedate and domestic Howellsian heroines.

Arguing in fiction and in articles in popular magazines against
the restrictions on women's development caused by a belief in
romantic love, [26] Mrs. Atherton lamented that "the exigencies of
civilization demanded an unequal development" of the physical
and mental capabilities of men and women. The new circumstances that allowed widening opportunities for the leisured
middle-class woman caused Mrs. Atherton to wonder in 1909
why love continued to be the principal theme of the novel. She
believed that only an objective and original woman writer would
and could carry the development of a type of aspiring woman
character to a logical conclusion, which might or might not
include love and marriage; only such a woman writer would
resist the temptation to conventionalize her heroine and would
build her identity independent of but similar to the nature of
man. With her view of affinity at the core of reality, Mrs.
Atherton in her novels redefined woman's part in affinity and
presented a psychological drama of a woman's quest for identity
and for a life purpose within and beyond her procreative
function. In *Ancestors* (1907), Isabel Otis pursues her independent life until her love for Jack Gwynne, developed by friendship
and common interests, convinces her that marriage will bring
happiness without loss of individuality. This plan of life,
originating in natural forces and social custom, in part explained
Mrs. Atherton's romantic realism as a union of a woman's
aspiration and the exigencies of civilization.[27]

The California author's resistance to portraying in her novels a
traditional affinity and her insistence that the novel should have
a form and style compatible with its theme account in part for

her narrative strengths and weaknesses. The structure of her
novels rests on her thematic plan of life. Her characters mirror
the effects of their expected social roles, and their reactions in
turn become causes that affect other characters and the social
structure. The characterization of an independent, self-knowing
woman, for instance, would require a description of the reactions
of a traditional man to her and a notation of any change in him.
When critics noted a separation between Mrs. Atherton's general
theme and the particular circumstances portrayed and complained about a prolix style, [28] they failed to recognize that the
logic of her characters' series of actions and reactions within
their plan of life required expanded explanation. When Mrs.
Atherton contrasted American and English attitudes on the
relation between the sexes, as in *American Wives and English
Husbands* (1898), the story had two parts—one delineating each
position. When she dealt with the initiation of a woman into
maturity in the 488 pages of *Patience Sparhawk and Her Times*
(1897), the five parts of the story represented the stages of
Patience's development from an isolated childhood on a
California ranch to multiple adventures in the highly organized
society in New York.[29] Since many of Patience's ideas and
adventures were unusual for a woman in the 1890s, the author
had to provide the context of the times to support them.
Attempting to move her heroines in later novels, such as *The
Sisters-in-Law* (1921) and *The House of Lee* (1940), into the
mainstream of rapidly changing circumstances and beliefs
between two world wars, Mrs. Atherton still had to supply a
woman's view of these changes, but the acceptance of women's
increased activity enabled her to reduce the amount of narrative
exposition.

III   *The Audience: "There are Publics"*

Mrs. Atherton agreed with the results of a survey made by the
New York Public Library in 1916 that a typical American novel
could never be written because the United States was a "loose
bunch of nations," every state being different, so that a novel
attempting to depict so broad and various a nation would be
"long and laborious."[30] In 1935, listing contrasting types of fiction
and claiming that each found a band of followers, she explained a
cause-effect relationship in the variety of readers and the forms
of storytelling:

Historical novels, past and present, novels concentrated on men and women of high breeding and inherited position, on the small town, the middle-class, the proletariat; on current economic developments as they affect the individual or group; the regional novel with or without a universal application; that lucrative variety that can only be characterized as Mush for Morons; the calorific, so popular with the inquisitive young, and drab women; the detective-mystery-crime story beloved of all grades from master to butler, from professor to freshman. Well has it been said: there is no Public, there are publics. All these contrastive types of fiction find, in varying degrees, a place and a band of followers. Judging by occasional supersales, certain novels please all the publics; which merely prove that the general public is subject at times to one more mass impulse, or that intelligent persons like variety.[31]

Like Henry James, Gertrude Atherton analyzed the reading audience, found it diverse but also responsive to the concerns of a spiritual Young Person;[32] and recognized a particular segment, the increasing number of readers among middle-class women, that would be attracted to her fictional concerns. Her analysis also made her call for a more discerning corps of reviewers whose studied response to books, rather than an "individual opinion," would assist authors in their art.[33]

She immediately began both to utilize and to criticize this author-reader relationship in order to build and to maintain her literary career. In several articles, she severely criticized American readers, [34] and she directed her comments to a general rather than to an aesthetic relationship between reader and author. The undisciplined or "fugitive state" of book criticism she blamed on the proliferation of books to be reviewed, on the tendency of reviewers to approve the writer and a type of writing which had become familiar, and on the assignment of review books to overworked official readers and to less busy but critically ignorant members of the press. She also noted that long experience in book-reviewing resulted in a conservatism that resisted and resented any new or strong style or any different attitude toward the central problems of life.[35]

To remedy this static state of criticism, Mrs. Atherton urged authors to criticize each other's works and critics to observe "the rigid rules laid down by Sainte-Beuve." Then, she contended, critics would train their minds to criticism as the artist educates himself in the art to which he was born, or to which he elects himself. Following Sainte-Beuve, Mrs. Atherton separated the

critic and the imaginative writer: "The function of the critic is to
educate, to admonish, out of a large and conscientiously acquired
knowledge, unclouded by the vagaries of the creative mind, or
any sort of prejudice."[36] Although she frequently wrote book
reviews, Mrs. Atherton claimed that her creative imagination
prevented her from maintaining Sainte-Beuve's objectivity. The
talent of the creative writer causes a narrow vision and an
inclination toward prejudice, she wrote, while the education of
an objective critical mind produces a cold, detached judgment
proper to the criticism of authors. In reviewing May Sinclair's
biographical novel *Mary Oliver* in 1919, Mrs. Atherton declined
to "criticize" the work of an already established writer and
instead described how she felt and thought about Sinclair and
her ideas in the novel.[37] Through her book reviews, Mrs.
Atherton revealed enough of her reaction to reviewers' thoughts
about her work to indicate that she primarily wanted to know
whether or not the reader or critic enjoyed her book; this is an
expected response, in view of her interest in entertaining and
extending the world of the reader.

In regard to her American audience, Mrs. Atherton agreed
with James's description of the public for literature as one
"subdivided as a chessboard, with each little square confessing
only to its own kind of accessibility."[38] In 1901 she wrote, "The
truth is there are as many separate publics for as many varieties
of the novel as can be devised," and readers are "sometimes
unreasonably exacting and sometimes not, just as they are
sometimes prudish and sometimes not."[39] She tried to counter
the readers' inconsistency. She declared that the images of an
author could not affect the morality of a young (usually female)
reader, who needed the concreteness of textbook facts and
parlance if she were to modify her behavior.[40] In *Patience
Sparhawk* and *The Californians*, the young heroines who read
many books find literature no guide for living their lives or facing
their problems. Furthermore, recognizing that promiscuous
reading of novels is a form of killing time and escaping dull
existences, Mrs. Atherton praised "lesser" middle-class women
and working women for reading the historical romances of
Winston Churchill, Paul Leicester Ford, and Mary Johnston as a
means of learning history and ideas not familiar to them.[41]
Although she decried the insatiable demand of the ever-
increasing numbers of readers as responsible for the publication

of bad and good books, thereby decreasing the opportunity for an aristocracy of letters, Gertrude Atherton claimed that she continued to give her set of readers "a diet worthy of a virile hungry mind."[42]

A few reviewers complained that Mrs. Atherton did not respect the intelligence of the reading audience; others tried to assess her audience objectively; one reviewer remarked that bad reviews did not affect her book sales because of the fidelity of her own set of readers.[43] In 1918, Grant Overton described her public as composed of those who were "capable of some degree of purely aesthetic enjoyment in literature" and others who did not ask fiction to interpret them to themselves or to shape their lives consciously or otherwise.[44] *Patience Sparhawk,* however, achieved an enduring reputation as an impetus to the spirit of independence of women through two decades of sales (pp. 252, 267), and *Black Oxen* lifted the spirits of women in their middle years (pp. 560-62). In 1929, Lionel Stevenson, echoed by Kevin Starr in 1973, defined Mrs. Atherton's audience as falling between contempt of Edgar Rice Burroughs and admiration for the refinements of Henry James because of their lowbrow desire for spiciness and melodrama and their highbrow aspirations to discuss and analyze theories of psychology.[45]

IV   Character: "Living Realities . . . Dissevered from the Page"

Because she considered that the adventure of writing was an adventure of the mind only, Gertrude Atherton was frequently asked how she wrote fiction. Her novel began, she replied, with a motive, a *mis-en-scène,* and a character or characters who had been clamoring for some time in her fictional tract and demanding to be let out.[46] The American novelist, she continued, is driven to psychology, a study of the inner life of characters that will reveal the peaks and valleys of life which are often obscured to the reader of Realistic fiction. Such an inward turn of mind produced for her living novel "characters . . . so powerfully realized and presented that they dissever themselves from the page" and are perceived by the reader as vividly as any of his acquaintances in the flesh.[47]

Mrs. Atherton developed her characters by what they did and by how they reacted to their own actions and those of others. These reactions might have either minor or startling results, but the actions and reactions always carried both characters and story a step, or a leap, forward. This was her conception of development of character and story by action, the working of "the immutable law of cause and effect," even if the action were "skull-bound" and had "nothing in common with visible causations." Hence she told her story often through mental monologues in which the characters reflected on their feelings and actions as well as through dramatized external conflicts.[48]

How did she select characters and make them live? Mrs. Atherton derived from Hippolyte Taine her method of lifting a type of man or woman out of the commonplace conditions to which either is apparently doomed and transferring him or her to an environment replete with change and opportunity where any latent potentialities and his or her own purpose in life can be developed.[49] Each type of character is affected, as Taine indicates, by "heredity, early regional fate, family influences, too much affection or too little—all the forces that swirl about childhood," all of which influence the individual's efforts to remold himself in respect to his own discovered life goal.

As a result, Mrs. Atherton thought of a character's total personality as an envelope that is either self-created or results from the sum of his or her inheritances and experiences in a particular environment.[50] She was concerned with passionate natures living in environments where passions are depressed or diverted from their natural courses. She wanted to express the variability of a woman's nature and its similarity in some respects to that of a man. She insisted that a woman could develop her will and intellect in order to build her own self-concept despite the effect of heredity and of social and physical forces on her. Hence the intellectual siren, the passionate middle-aged woman, and the romantic egoist are familiar types that Mrs. Atherton consistently lifted out of their restricting environments and permitted to develop elsewhere.

Believing with Taine that literature was a transcription of contemporary manners and that behind each work was a genuine "underworld of a person," Mrs. Atherton thought that the writer and a character in a novel logically acted out their inherited and acquired traits and circumstances, whether beneficial or inimical. The result is the novel that consists of the logical development of the plan of life of a type of character. In an era in which the dominant place of man was being challenged by the awakening woman, Gertrude Atherton's women and men offered a different view of the human race and its progress. She only generally discussed her types of characters, but she admitted that "the difficult part of writing is the selection of types and placing them without prejudice in their true environment."[51] She discovered similar types of characters in different countries and races, for she believed that perceived differences in human motives were universal, the differences originating in universal emotions rather than in national conditions. Most of her types she developed from the personalities of living persons, selecting them from the contemporary "whole sentiment of life in America." Hence she portrayed the small-town character, the older woman, the homely woman, the aspiring type, the ideal, the languid, the arrogant, the ambitious.

An interviewer of Gertrude Atherton in 1917 described her character types in each decade as standing for progress, foresight, and truth. "The element of irony in my nature," she told the interviewer, "is inevitably opposed to looking backward, to seeing the things and the people around me with the sentimentality of a former generation."[52] She excepted from this antipathy such heroic types of the past as Alexander Hamilton, Aspasia, and Dido, about whom she wrote novels. Even the short story, she said, standardized newly developing American types. However, as she observed the changing conditions in Europe and America, even her old types—of women in particular—became to her like "photos in an old album stiffly posed and out of date." A new type of matured woman, and a man to match her expectations, she began to describe in fiction and essays at the turn of the century and again just before World War I.[53] She portrayed the independent, educated will of woman, her power in the family, the power struggle of husband and wife and its effect on children and even a possible new kind of woman's heroine—an "intermediate sex"[54] exemplified by Helena Belmont of *The Californians* (1898), Marguerite Styr of *Tower of Ivory* (1910), and Ora Stratton of *Perch of the Devil* (1914)—who cherishes an ideal rather than a real mate and remains single—as well as older women, such as Mrs.. Edington and Mrs. Lee in *The House of Lee* (1940), who choose an active, self-supporting widowhood rather than security with a man. In these characterizations, Mrs. Atherton emphasized the variety of women's temperaments and choices of life purposes.

Because Gertrude Atherton's belief in progress was balanced by her acknowledgement that human nature does not change, she could not entirely resolve the question of the relation of heredity and environment to character. Aristocracy and democracy, class and race, talent and temperament, energy and inertia—all offer different possibilities to different types of characters. In *Ancestors* (1907), a titled Englishman because of his American birth, can work out his own political destiny either in England or in California, while the California heroine of the novel develops her inherited abilities and a life purpose in the state of her birth by transforming this Englishman into an American. In 1913, Mrs. Atherton expressed a belief that the awakening of women to the pursuit of their own happiness is the real birth of democracy.[55] By 1940, she could imagine in *The House of Lee* (1940) three generations of California women who are prepared by their independent spirit to handle their drastically reduced financial circumstances and who by assessing their own abilities to support themselves can choose to work as well to consider security in some kind of liaison with a man. In these independent types, Mrs. Atherton expressed her sense that Western civilization had responded to human aspiration by recognizing the merit of individual achievement while preserving the notion of an exceptional social group, a new aristocracy that valued intellect, talent, and ability regardless of class.

The presentation of those three generations in *The House of Lee* illustrates Mrs. Atherton's concern for the connection between characterization and the form and structure of fiction. In separate chapters, each woman reveals her real self in her boudoir mirror and in her public actions. Although the author relied on a novelist's instinct to select an appropriate form and style for each novel, she almost always chose an omniscient narrator to tell the story from some limiting perspective, most often that of the major character but frequently that of two or more characters. Only in *The Doomswoman* (1893), the novel with which Mrs. Atherton declared her literary career began, and *Golden Peacock* (1936) did she employ a first-person narrator. The audacious, self-confident sixteen-year-old Pomponia in the latter novel, discovering and resolving the scheme to assassinate Augustus, keeps the plot of the novel under control; whereas the first-person narrator in *The Doomswoman*, though a confidante of the protagonist, does not seem deeply enough involved in the conflict to provide a credible intensity that the tragic story requires.

The omniscient narrator most effectively served Mrs. Atherton's intention to explore—and then to affect the reader's response to—the inner life and the extraneous circumstances and reactions of her various types of characters. In the early novels, the narrator relates the long conversations of the main characters, usually a man and a woman; the conversations allow the woman's ideas to be developed and to be evaluated by a man, a respectful listener. The man functions as a reflector rather than the focus of the major point of view, a reversal of the usual male role in fiction. In addition to the record of these discussions, the author includes many descriptive details concerning the characters' clothing, facial expressions, and emotions. This diffuseness caused some readers and reviewers to complain about too many ideas being expressed in one novel and too much separation between the center of the novel and its supportive details. In support of her digressions, Mrs. Atherton criticized both the narrowness of Sinclair Lewis's vision of a small town's smug morality in *Main Street* and Edith Wharton's depiction of only a fragment of New York society in *The House of Mirth*.[56]

Consistent with her intention to be a "correct historian" of her own times, Mrs. Atherton also has her narrator function as a central intelligence linking the contemporary times of the reader and the time in the story. Her biographical novels exemplify her skill and wit in comparing the past and the present. In her presentation of Alexander Hamilton in *The Conqueror*, she has the narrator comment on current political and social events as outcomes of and contrasts to the ideas and actions of Hamilton and his times. Mrs. Atherton insisted that a novel's motif be placed in a context of human nature in its infinite variety. Hence her narrator's presentation of tangential subplots and discourses of the characters integrate the plan of life in the novel.

V   *Style and Technique: "My Style Is My Own"*

As in all of her commentary on the art of fiction and the craft of writing, Gertrude Atherton expressed opinions on style and technique in terms of her perception of the chasm between two literary standards—that of the imaginative, original writer and that of the "thin" Realistic and magazine-school author. The first, she said, appealed to the readers' hunger for knowledge of the great world beyond their own, and the second to the bourgeois or middle-class mentality that preferred to view the world as it ought to be rather than as it is. This two-pronged appeal distinguished the audience of near-intellectuals from that of the readers of best-sellers toward whom Mrs. Atherton turned her attention after 1914.

Describing what she believed style ought to be, Mrs. Atherton complained of the grammatical offenses, dialect, and local color in magazine fiction and of the "narrow, finicky, commonplace" style of the Howells school. In these comments, she was apparently objecting to the ideas that the style of writing reflected. She further illustrated her animus against the sameness of the Realistic style by her reference to a composite novel suggested by Howells in 1907. This novel was composed of chapters written by different authors. Asked to contribute a chapter to this novel, Mrs. Atherton read several chapters preceding the one she was to write. When she could not distinguish the style of one chapter from another, "so beautifully alike, such faultless specimens of our American magazine school," she declined to participate in the "indefective writing" that, in her opinion, passed for style in the United States.[57]

Without explaining the adjectives she used, Mrs. Atherton differentiated several other aspects of style. To handle such interdicted subjects as sexuality and love scenes, she saw a need for an "impersonal cold style" such as that of Flaubert in *Madame Bovary* and of Balzac, whose language, she said, had a flexibility and grace that English as a language lacked. She also praised the hard "cold brilliancy" of Edith Wharton's depiction of the "merest fragment" of New York society in *The House of Mirth* (1905), but she added that a great American novel, dealing with the life of New York in the comprehensive masterly style heretofore lacking in the best-sellers, had yet to be written.[58] Mrs. Atherton's style for an all-around American love scene, which she declared American fiction lacked, first appeared in *A Whirl Asunder* (1895), in which the lovers disappeared into the redwood forest, sat on a log, and made conversation.[59] The passion portrayed, being intellectual as well as physical, represented Mrs. Atherton's attempt to modify the stereotype of woman as a mere physical object and to entertain her readers by not fulfilling their expectations of sentimental and romantic details.

Gertrude Atherton's most specific comment about the source of her own style appeared in her autobiography. Shortly before his death in 1898, Harold Frederic had praised her lucidity of style and claimed for her a clearer vocation to write novels than for any other woman he knew:

> I should harangue you about the peril, not perhaps of writing too much, but of writing too easily. You have in an extreme degree the talent of lucidity—but melody is an acquired gift with all but the laurel-wreathed few. Do take the pace a little more slowly, and listen with a more solicitous reflective ear—and get the trick of drawing sound out of the ink bottle . . . but if you write "United Statesian" and things like that, the critics will never find themselves realizing this truth.

Mrs. Atherton reported that she followed his advice "sometimes":

> Style is a matter of temperament, and unless one is cool and placid and suave by nature, or devoted to one ideal only, one cannot preserve a uniform style in writing. Herbert Spencer is difficult reading himself, and less for content than manner, but he wrote a valuable essay on style, and the admonition that made the deepest impression on me . . . was that style should vary with the subject. (pp. 313-14)

The evidence of her interpretation of Spencer lies in her sometimes unusual diction, her use of slang, and even her frequently turgid sentences and confusing arrangement of incidents.[60]

Believing that a style applied uniformly to every phase and mood of a story would be a sign of timidity and a poverty of imaginative resources, Mrs. Atherton followed Rousseau's style in *The Confessions*, which she thought fitted style and tempo to the changing demands of the narrative.[61] "My style is my own," she declared,[62] and she gave each novel an inborn individuality and continued to select words and construct sentences that bothered critics and an older generation of novelists. The wit and humor and the lack of sentimentality that critics frequently identified in her work resulted from her independent attitude toward style and from her observation of different types of

characters and situations in American life that were not treated
by other writers.[63]

VI   The Act of Writing: "I Am a Wanderer"

Gertrude Atherton composed the first and third copy of most
of her novels on a typewriter. She wrote at a desk in pensions,
hotel rooms, and apartments in California, New York, and
Europe. "I have no home," she told Francis Halsey in 1903. "I am
a wanderer upon the face of the earth. Freedom is, or at least
should be, essential to any artist, and freedom is to be found only
through an open mind and a wide and varying horizon."[64]

A paragraph from her 1935 essay on imagination expresses
what Mrs. Atherton considered of great importance in storytelling:

Save for a few amateur performances, which I ignore, I began by
writing historical novels and stories, even if only of the preceding
generation—for those at least were social history—and had every
intention of doing nothing else. I like the perspective, the research, the
re-creation of a past era. But partly because someone piqued me by
saying that I was not in tune with my own times and never could be:
that I was born too late or too soon; partly because in due course, that is
to say in a wider experience of life, contemporaneous stories would
suddenly begin to prowl about my fiction tract; partly because earlier
in my career not enough historical characters appealed to me—there
was an interval of four years between "The Conqueror" and
"Rezánov," and then nineteen years passed before "The Immortal
Marriage"—just about half of my output has dealt with the passing
scene. Even so, I have been accused of making my contemporary
heroines "superwoman"—although what my critics meant was un-
ordinary—just as I chose superwomen of history, like Aspasia, to
resurrect. Well, I hate commonplace persons both in fiction and out.
. . . What I am looking for is more superwomen in history.[65]

Gertrude Atherton respected the past as an exercise for the
imagination, but she lived primarily in the present state of
humanity and took its pulse to tell stories about it and to envision
its future. Her various apartments had no attics in which she
could store the artifacts of her sixty years of writing, yet she
trusted that the ideas and novelties of the past would recur in the
present for her to treat again. An overview of her career

demonstrates the constant recycling of her major interests as a storyteller—the examination of the romantic-realistic pursuit of happiness through individual achievement, the transformation of types of people and of historical characters in fictional circumstances, the description of cultural novelties appealing to a middle-class audience, and the eager observation of the procession of Western civilization.

CHAPTER 3

Romantic Realism: A Western Pursuit of Happiness

G ERTRUDE Atherton's apprentice work extended from 1888 to 1895, though she claimed that her literary career began with *The Doomswoman* (1893). In this period, she sought expression for the confused feelings and thoughts about individual fate that had originated in her undisciplined youth and in her wide but untutored reading. Uncertain how to express her untraditional characters' quests for happiness in a late nineteenth-century literary world, she created self-conflicted characters, romantically striving toward an ideal but confronting the realities of their times and gaining knowledge of themselves. By employing in her early short stories and short novels her knowledge of the past and present of California and of San Francisco to create her *mis-en-scène,* she practiced ways to control the incidents growing out of the ideas and emotions of her aspiring characters.

Her first three California novels and her collection of short stories reveal her ability to tell a compelling tale and to capture the California historical scene and arcadian atmosphere. They also show her tendency to produce melodrama by narrating in declaimed monologues and stilted conversation and to use diction for startling effect. In *Los Cerritos: A Romance of the Modern Time* (1890), an unsophisticated daughter of a California bandit, melodramatically escaping poverty through marriage to a wealthy landowner, discourses with her lover on the problem of the rich and the poor in America—one of Atherton's concerns. *The Doomswoman* (1893) grounds the characterization of self-conflicted Chonita Moncada y Iturbi in an old Spanish legend, which gives a woman, who is a twin, a paradoxical power to heal and curse and to give and know the highest joy and sorrow. This characterization, accomplished through the heroine's monologues of self-explanation and her empathetic conversations with her lover, makes predictable the tragic death of Chonita and her lover, who dreams of modernizing California. The eleven stories of *Before the Gringo Came* (1894), though theatrical and sketchy, vividly recreate the lost California Arcadia of the "splendid idle 1840s," especially from the point of view of the women's reaction to the customs of that time. *A Whirl Asunder* (1895) presents Helena Belmont as Mrs. Atherton's California prototype of woman, combining a Byronic romantic ego, the intellect of Madame de Staël's Corinne, and a Paterlike idealism. Helena Belmont pursues happiness in the form of an ideal man by becoming engaged many times, and she suffers grandly when the ideal she finds, an English barrister, chooses to marry a typical Englishwoman.

The ambiguous happiness that the California heroines achieve in marriage or in idealism did not resolve Mrs. Atherton's uncertain romantic-realistic intention to explore the pursuit of happiness of man and woman. The characters are more abstract than real; they espouse their feelings and thoughts in unspoken soliloquies, and the incidents sometimes lack connection with each other. Yet her depiction of the scene and milieu drew readers to these stories of beautiful, aggrandizing, expanding California in the period between 1840 and 1890. One day, Mrs. Atherton wrote in her autobiography (pp. 224-25),[1] a "distinctive heroine" walked into her fictional tract; determined to write this character's romantic-realistic life history, the novelist discovered her creative faculty bursting forth "like a geyser, and accumulated experience, impressions, rebellions, deductions poured forth." Patience Sparhawk was the first of five distinctive heroines to escape from a personal psychological "fool's paradise" in the context of California as the Western "fool's paradise" of European civilization. Their stories, written between 1897 and 1907, began Mrs. Atherton's social history of California, a wider project that extended to 1942.

I Patience Sparhawk and Her Times:
"The Spirit of Feminine Revolt"

Patience Sparhawk and Her Times (1897) relates the "times" of the heroine's youth on a poverty-stricken ranch near Monterey, California, in the 1880s and her education in a small town on the Hudson River and in the New York City of the 1890s. A passionate and willful girl, Patience spends a lonely youth, her nature and social opportunities repressed by her poor environment and by her alcoholic mother's neglect. Patience is the first of the group of characters for whom Mrs. Atherton preferred to create a different set of circumstances and an environment that would develop her potentialities beyond the capacity of her origins.

In *Patience Sparhawk*, Gertrude Atherton achieves a more realistic characterization of her aspiring heroine than she had managed before. Patience's mental attitudes are as important as external circumstances in effecting her rise from poverty to the status of a self-respecting gentlewoman. Mrs. Atherton focuses on a few crucial years in Patience's early womanhood, elaborates a single psychological conflict, observes minor characters and their environment minutely, and concentrates on Patience's view of herself. Several themes underlie the mental and external action: the effect of social class and circumstances on individual will and passion; the human nature of woman; and the basis of a happy marriage. Patience's unspoken analyses of human behavior and her thoughts on religion, literature, and an ideal mate crowd the novel with apparently extraneous matter that is difficult to summarize; but these also reveal the inner confusion of a young woman coming to terms with both illusive romantic ideals and the practical realities of sexuality and an independent purpose in life. Mrs. Atherton's consistently ironic view of Patience's conflict makes credible her characterization of a willfully vain and aspiring woman in the 1890s. In this work, the author for the first time exemplifies her definition of the novel— the plan of life, the characterization, and the series of incidents are caused by mental attitudes as much as by external forces.

Patience's higher goal and gradual rise through social classes depend on her peculiarly American "individual Will" and "larger faculties," which, according to Mrs. Atherton's borrowing of Paul Bourget's opinion,[2] predicted a higher civilization or chaos. As a social historian, Mrs. Atherton carries Patience's aspiration to its logical end through all the psychological barriers and social attitudes that an assertive and confused young middle-class woman would confront at the time.[3]

As a ranch girl, envious of and ignored by her more fortunate classmates, Patience compensates for her loneliness by reading, by competing for grades in school, and by aspiring to an ideal individuality beyond her surroundings. Her use of will and mental ability to improve her circumstances, however, is restricted by her mother's promiscuous behavior. Enraged one day, Patience willfully attacks her mother and enjoys the horror of the ranch hands who witness her assault. So Patience early recognizes the duality of human nature: the forces of will and passion can cause one to rise or fall according to the way one reacts to them, and one can count on overreacting and deluding oneself.

Away from California, Patience finds herself beginning to oscillate between the guidance of her brain and the chaos of emotions, and between her rise in social class and her consciousness of the base and high motivations in each class— about which she attempts to maintain an amused and detached attitude. Influenced by the manners and affection of her spinster "auntie," Miss Tremont, in the religious and moral community of Mariaville, Patience gains control of her temper and learns social ease with the aristocratic Peeles. She is especially calmed by her friendship with "Hal" Peele, who warns her that no one can live fully on an ideal. She also becomes skeptical about Miss Tremont and Miss Beale, whose religious and temperance activities among the disadvantaged people of Mariaville appear to be a substitute for marriage. However, Patience's experience at this point does not provide her with a life purpose matching her aspiration or substituting for traditional matrimony. Awakened to her sexuality, which her brain and will are less able to control, Patience resists but resignedly accepts the approved channel for her passion—marriage to Beverly Peele.

In her new, leisurely, upper-class life at Peele Manor, Patience now has her dreamed-of status as a member of an elite group, even as she notes the "larky" adventures and ennui existing in it. Eventually she discovers that her will cannot force her mind and emotions to endure marriage in which she and Beverly do not develop beyond an external and physical relationship. Finally overcoming the fear of scandal and failure because of her dissatisfaction with her marriage, Patience leaves Peele Manor and attempts to support herself in the newspaper world. Though tired and poor, she enjoys friendship with a fellow reporter, Miss Merrien, and learns more about human relationships from Morgan Steele, the editor of the *New York Day*. Perversely delighted in attracting him, Patience nevertheless rejects his proposal of a "comfortable state" between them "with plenty of brains, philosophy and passion" and no illusions. Ignoring her knowledge of other people's failures with idealism, Patience offers him a feeble but romantic excuse that "like and passion" do not constitute an ideal love that is capable of a "splendid self-sacrifice" (pp. 406-407).

When Beverly Peele is found dead by poison, Patience is arrested. In prison, facing trial and then execution, she summons all of her will, education and aristocratic manner to maintain her courage and dignity and to face death as a "gentlewoman." Yet her conviction causes her aristocratic ego to rage against the jury of small-town citizens who, she believes, have convicted her because of her independent personality, her lack of religious belief, and her enviable social status. Forgetful of her humble origin, Patience, like Madame de Staël's Corrine, voices the pride and penalty of the elite. Her plight, however, reunites her with her youthful ideal, Garan Bourke, now a New York lawyer; he defends her, melodramatically rescues her from the electric chair at the last moment, and offers her the union of mind and spirit in marriage which she has long been seeking.

Patience's rise from the ignominy of poverty and degradation to the self-pride of an aristocratic type is described rather than analyzed. Incidents follow each other without visible reason because Patience primarily reacts to what she thinks about her circumstances rather than rebelling against them in order to take charge of her life. She observes her emotions and ideas, and, candidly acknowledging that the imp of the perverse operates in her nature, takes pleasure in forcing people to respond to her sexual and intellectual magnetism. Patience never outgrows her need to be admired. Still, she overflows with more energy and interest in life than the typical heroines of the Realistic school. Although her creator denied that in her characterization of Patience she expressed "the general revolt of women against the tyranny of man and his self-made world," many of the minor characters, such as Miss Tremont, Hal Peele, and Miss Merrien, also represent the restrictive effects of social custom on women; and Patience does not find happiness in woman's expected destiny until the end of the novel.

The melodramatic elements in the plot and Patience's high-flown rhetoric on creative force and spirituality reflect Mrs. Atherton's perception of what appealed to her audience. Beneath the plot and rhetoric lies the author's effort to extend her middle-class readers' knowledge of the "times" by dramatizing the ideas and attitudes she observed in American society in the 1890s. Various characterizations reflect such social topics as the use of time and money, the distrust of different classes for each other, the various kinds of marriage, and the possibility of a new type of American woman.

In this novel, the social class and source of money of the various characters affect the way they make use of time in carrying out their life purposes. Patience observes that Miss Tremont and Miss Beale, financially independent religious altruists, invest their time and money among the poor and the alcoholic, probably as an expression of their need to exercise power and to love. Some leisured wives of well-to-do landowners on the Hudson River, on the other hand, accept a passionless marriage and merely write checks to the pastor to fulfull the wealthy class's obligation to the poor (p. 205). Working people such as Miss Merrien and the hard-featured, middle-aged jurors at Patience's trial view with envy the apparent ease of the well-to-do, while the wealthy, especially the wives—whose leisure is purchased by their husbands' efforts—insist that the lower class has no ground for grumbling about leisure time. Possessing all of a leisured wife's advantages except money of her own, Patience chafes at the necessity of having to ask her husband for money; and her small inheritance from Miss Tremont becomes the first means by which she can leave her psychological uncertainty and economic dependence on her husband and by her own effort achieve a balance between self-reliance and her need for companionship. In these characterizations and incidents, Mrs. Atherton fictionally portrays the later observations of Charlotte Perkins Gilman in *Women and Economics* (1898) and Thorstein Veblen in *The Theory of the Leisure Class* (1899).

The circumstances of Patience's isolated childhood, which tend to distort her perception of woman's nature and of the relationship between man and woman, reflect isolation of the nineteenth-century woman from the mainstream of American life. On their passage to New York, Mr. Fields predicts that Patience's common sense will reveal "several eternal truths"

about the nature of women (p. 86). Patience's later experiences
confirm such truths as a woman's strong sexual nature, the
disassociation of love and sex, and woman's inherited "instinct of
dependence on man" and a "sexual horror of the arena" of
competition that leads her passively to accept marriage (p. 239).[4]

The nineteenth-century separation of the roles of men and
women and the competition among women for possession of a
man in marriage account in part for Patience's observations of
the various kinds of American marriages. She excoriates the "free-
love" relationship with men exemplified by her mother and by
her childhood friend, Rosita Thrailkill, who becomes a mistress
of a theatrical producer in order to promote her career and to
live luxuriously. On the other hand, Patience and her lover,
Garan Bourke, regard as harlotry the upper-class marriage of
convenience or a woman's remaining married to a man she does
not love. Hal Peele, Patience's sister-in-law, represents the
dilemma of the upper-class woman: she credibly displays her
anguish in deciding not to marry the poorer man whom she loves,
in order to maintain her luxurious existence in marriage to a
wealthy man. Hal, like Patience, articulates the human dilemma
of having to deal with the Law of Circumstance by some
acceptance of the Law of Compensation (p. 232). The tragedy
possible in woman's having to find her existence primarily in a
man's love is portrayed by Honora Mairs, the adopted orphan
cousin of Hal and Beverly Peele. In their house, Honora early
learns the lesson that if she is to gain a supportable position in life
she must manipulate people tactfully and repress her own
desires. Loving Beverly Peele, Honora watches Patience marry
him and then leave him; it is she who actually poisons him
because she cannot have him and because she wants to save him
from Patience.

The types of men who love and admire Patience Sparhawk in
their own fashion mirror the effect on men generally of the
customs of courtship and marriage. Beverly Peele, probably
modeled after Mrs. Atherton's husband, is characterized as
entirely physical in nature, spoiled by his mother, and unable to
relate maturely to others. Less individualistic than representative of their function as mentors of Patience and reflectors of her
ideas are Mr. Field, a New York publisher, Morgan Steele, and
Garan Bourke. They are not "flat" characters, but are described
rather as successful men who admire and make credible the

"larger more human type" of woman, like Patience, who will found a "new race" (p. 201) and contrast with the New York girl of Henry James and Edith Wharton. The men also represent Mrs. Atherton's ideas of the types of new men who will match the expectations of the new, self-reliant, sexually and intellectually assertive woman, who needs a spiritual and mental equal in marriage.

When Gertrude Atherton fills this novel with "accumulated experiences, impressions, rebellions, deductions," she does so to portray the psychological uncertainty and social difficulties against which Patience reacts. The novelist synthesizes this turmoil through a unified point of view to the extent that Patience observes mentally each segment of her experience. Some segments and Patience's reaction to them are also filtered through the eyes of another person. This technique helps to define the observer, a character such as Morgan Steele or Hal Peele, by contrasting his or her outlook and behavior with that of Patience. This contrast provides a witty correction of Patience's "anarchic theories" on religion, on clever women, and on remorseless murder (pp. 236-37).

Gertrude Atherton's evocation of setting enhances her characterization of Patience and her times. The poverty of the California ranch and its isolation from the Eastern mecca serve as an effective stage from which to emancipate Patience Sparhawk. The introspective Patience blossoms first in the close-knit community and in the woods around Mariaville, whose beauty contrasts favorably with her memories of California's ocean and redwoods. Realistic details of parties, costumes, and conversation at Peele Manor support Patience's emergence as a refined gentlewoman, while the tense drama of the courtroom, sparked by the contrast between the romantic, aristocratic lawyer and the prosaic jurors, representing the people, is a highly realistic picture of the judicial system. Mrs. Atherton's use of the imagery of rain to evoke Patience's memories of significant events in her life at the moment of her impending execution effectively mixes the terror of her situation with her will to face her fate courageously.

Mrs. Atherton improved her style in *Patience Sparhawk*, which marked her advance as a professional novelist. Her narration carries the reader through the five parts of the novel by adapting its pace to the sense of time needed to portray the stages of

Patience's development toward the climax of her journey. Now and then appear epigrammatic observations on the world from a woman's point of view, and these contrast effectively with the soliloquies and opinions expressed by the major characters. She attempts to record modern slang in Hal Peele's speech, and sometimes disrupts the reader's expectations with her own coinages such as "United Statesian" (in the epigraph), "brainy" (p. 87), and "blondinity" (p. 218). The momentum that Mrs. Atherton generated in this novel resulted in a series that comprises a story-chronicle of California from the 1840s to the 1940s.

II   The Californians: *"A Good Deal of Tragedy in California"*

In *The Californians* (1898) Gertrude Atherton tells the story of a different type of aspiring California heroine. Romantic in its depiction of an ambitious state and of shy Magdalena Yorba's desire to become a writer, the novel also provides a Realistic account of San Francisco in the 1880s. As Mrs. Atherton wrote of the potentialities of California and San Francisco, she was conscious of the play of cause and effect in the greed, ambition, and corruption that accompany expansion, and she narrated the effect of falling fortunes on the families of an Old Spanish Grandee, a Southern cavalry officer, and a Yankee trader, all of whom had seized the opportunity for wealth in California but had lost the traditional values associated with their origins.

Mrs. Atherton's novel depicts an aspect of the California story untouched by other California writers, such as Bret Harte. It focuses on the intertwined fates of the inhabitants of mansions built on Nob Hill by three families: Don Roberto, his Yankee wife, Hannah, sister of Hiram Polk, and their plain-faced daughter, Magdalena; Colonel Jack Belmont, his Boston-bred wife, and their beautiful, willful daughter, Helena; and Hiram Polk and his wife, Magdalena, sister of Don Roberto. Spanish pride, Southern manners, and Yankee shrewdness combine to produce wealth, but their ambition and greed preclude other possibilities, like public service or personal and familial happiness. The Nob Hill residents inhabit a "fool's paradise," able to see only the beauty of sky, ocean, and exclusive friendships, and they ignore the realities below them on the wharf, in Spanish and China towns, and in the hustling city. The Californians' inbred society prescribes personal goals and relationships that debase a secretive individual like Magdalena Yorba and enhance a typical materialistic siren like Helena Belmont. The book gains significance from the implication that a human being can find a reason for living though suffering a near defeat in a society whose values are narrowly defined. As Magdalena moves toward tragedy, she gains an understanding of her own and others' disappointments and reveals that in essence she is superior to those who had put all their life purpose into society and wealth.

The main plot of the novel presents a romantic triangle involving Magdalena, Helena, and Jack Trennahan. Their peculiar egos—their personal "fool's paradises" that direct their reactions to the circumstances of California in the 1880s—show the author's further exploration of psychological realism. The focus of the novel is the gradual emergence of the soul of the introverted Magdalena from its entrapment in traditional beliefs and attitudes toward a realistic assessment of inner desire. The first book portrays the repressed emotions and thoughts of Magdalena that grope toward articulation and social ease, and her happy friendship with the adventurous Helena. Magdalena gains confidence from the sympathetic attention of Jack Trennahan, a "world-weary" Adam who in his own way is searching for a purposeful life. Trennahan thinks that in Magdalena he at last has found a peaceful love.

The second book delineates the falling fortunes of all the principals. Magdalena unselfishly breaks her engagement to Trennahan when she discovers that Helena and he believe that they are passionately in love. When Helena refuses to marry Trennahan after he confesses his previous experience with women, Magdalena, realizing her vain sacrifice, passionately but unsuccessfully assaults Helena. Trennahan exiles himself from "paradise," death comes to Hiram Polk and Colonel Belmont, and Don Roberto isolates himself in his sarcophagic mansion. Circumscribed by her father's demands and by her loss of Trennahan's love, Magdalena's will to face the reality of her life deteriorates; this decline, however, is abruptly climaxed by a second passionate awakening and by the return of Trennahan, rejuvenated by his having regained his earlier interest in a scientific career and seeking Magdalena's forgiveness. The suicide of Don Roberto, a symbolic act made concrete by his hanging himself with the American flag, releases Magdalena from her spiritual prison.

Mrs. Atherton's characterization of Magdalena Yorba gives

The Californians a timeless and universal appeal. Like every human being, Magdalena searches for a reason to be alive. Her social position secure as Patience Sparhawk's was not, Magdalena's search is primarily mental and emotional, more serious and complicated than that of her best friend, Helena, the willful "pagan" siren, who achieves easily what Magdalena thinks are her own desires. Magdalena and Helena are significantly named as inhabitants of a new-world Arcadia that inevitably must evolve into civilization. Able to integrate her New England assertiveness, her Southern charm, and her California "cheek," Helena becomes a "law" all to herself. In contrast, Magdalena's New England conscience and Spanish pride and faith for awhile override her California opportunities for developing her individuality. Gradually she moves through stages of understanding herself by outgrowing the restrictions inherent in her belief in the Virgin, in her duty to her father, and in the traditional role of woman. The contrast of Helena, the unchanging romantic ego, with Magdalena, freeing herself from dependence to self-reliance, is convincing because Mrs. Atherton has developed both types without judging either.

Magdalena gradually liberates herself from restrictive beliefs by her own presentiment of a higher destiny, but she does not lose her compassion for others. Her reactions to the people in her narrow environment and the effect of these reactions upon her personality tell the story of a young woman's initiation, a trial-and-error process of making her way through life, oscillating between passion and reticent pride, between secretiveness and yearning for attention, between aspiration and repression. She reaches a climactic resolution of her self-conflict in a Jungian night journey from her father's sarcophagus to a sexual awakening on the waterfront of San Francisco that forces her to "face her own soul" and to put her character together and willfully accept the future.

Don Roberto and Hiram Polk, partners in business who are also married to each other's sisters, and Colonel Belmont pursue wealth so ravenously that they alienate themselves from their own families and from wider social intercourse. Though Colonel Belmont is a dissipated hedonist, when science undermines Magdalena's religious belief she ironically turns to him rather than to her father or uncle for spiritual advice. The colonel recognizes that the repressed, passionate, intellectual Magdalena, unlike his daughter, Helena, might out of desperation be driven to "sudden extremes." As a substitute for her formal religion, he advises her to pursue an ideal, a desire for a concrete form of goodness to which she can cling when her human weakness or outside pressures overwhelm her. Thus aware of human weakness, Magdalena perceives her lonely Uncle Hiram's "hungry eyes" as he gazes upon party-goers and on his estranged wife as he lies dying. Don Roberto's pride in his success and his disdain of his daughter's love of books and the sacrifice of Trennahan to Helena drive him to reduce Magdalena and her mother to near poverty in a small part of the Nob Hill mansion and to isolate himself completely from them in his office. Idealistically defying his effort to force her to marry anyone against her will, Magdalena then devotes her energy to writing and to developing a warmer relationship with her mother. Mrs. Atherton's sympathetic characterizations make these three victims of greed more than types, because through them Magdalena sees their passionate greed as a tragedy of unfulfillment and vows to devote her life and her inheritance to aiding the poor.

Jack Trennahan is most significant in the novel for relating to Magdalena his conflict between an interest in scientific exploration and his choosing the upper-class pattern of pursuing women and power. In denying his own desire for a scientific career, Jack, like Magdalena, becomes vulnerable to sudden passionate extremes. In characterizing him, the author also wittily plays upon popular notions of the paradisical myth of regeneration and of the "goodness" of confession of past affairs. Self-centered Helena moralistically judges Trennahan because of his past behavior, while Magdalena is drawn to him in his desire to atone for his past wasted efforts by starting over again. One reviewer thought him unsubstantial in comparison to the "really vital creature," Magdalena, whose love of Jack humbles her pride.[5]

In *The Californians,* Gertrude Atherton establishes a greater distance from the central character than in *Patience Sparhawk,* and controls her multiplicity of impressions by selectively dramatizing several intense instances in Magdalena's development from self-sacrifice to self-assertion. Magdalena's interview with the worldly colonel, her efforts to make her pen write stories, her impulse to stab the fickle Helena, and her sexual awakening highlight the day-to-day pace of her initiation into selfhood in an arcadian land. Mrs. Atherton uses contrasting characters and scenes to balance one another, echoes earlier incidents late in the book, and quickly concludes her narrative after the climactic scene. In addition, she surrounds her characters with local color, integrating Spanish and American manners and morals and California scenery as a background for types of character new in American fiction. The candor, ready wit, and extravagances of expression of her California young women contrast not only with Magdalena's inarticulateness but also with the sedateness of the heroines of the Realistic school. She mythologizes a beautiful California as a Princess Royal of the United States who needs a tragic understanding before she can become "the most gracious mother mankind has ever known" (p. 171).

Mrs Atherton describes both the sunny and the seamy sides of San Francisco, and includes the people of the soil and the aliens, though less fully than the social set. As the focus of the novel, Magdalena Yorba's mental struggle in her original circumstances to find her own integrity and·to express in her life a compassion for others lifts *The Californians* beyond local color to make it one of Mrs. Atherton's best books, a novel of universal import and appeal.

III   American Wives and English Husbands:
"A Vein of Kindly Satire"

American Wives and English Husbands (1898) was Gertrude Atherton's first international novel with an independent California heroine who marries an upper-class Englishman. Henry James, reviewing her first international novel, *His Fortunate Grace* (1897), and this one, noted her satire of international marriage in the first novel, but declared that in the second one Mrs. Atherton had reduced the "great relation" of the sexes to differences in personality.[6] In the first part of *American Wives and English Husbands* Lee Tarleton develops her Western individuality in San Francisco in the 1880's, while in the second part she moves to the "grey imposing Fact" of England as the wife of an upper-class Englishman who expects her to become his second self. This novel continues Mrs. Atherton's fictional method of lifting a particular character out of her original environment and placing her in different circumstances—in this case, in American and English environments whose mores and attitudes affect her self-image and the relationship of the sexes.

The novel's first book introduces the two point-of-view characters on the periphery of San Francisco Society. Lee Tarleton and Cecil Maundrell find themselves in the same boardinghouse on Market Street in the roles of aristocrats "reduced" by financial reverses. Their friendship develops into an adolescent "engagement," but it is shifted to the background when the Maundrells, father and son, are recalled to England to take up residence in the supposedly cursed Maundrell Abbey, which the father has just inherited. A similar upswing in Lee's fortunes occurs at the death of her mother and upon her "adoption" into the socialite Montgomery family. In this family of Southern origin, Lee's submerged Creole heritage and Western individuality are developed and refined, and she gains a new dimension in learning how to manage her financial affairs.

Her "adopted" brother, Randolph Montgomery, the practical self-made American, vies with Cecil for Lee's love. In letters to Lee, Cecil reveals his intellectual initiation at Oxford and Balliol Colleges, so that when Cecil visits California again the stage is set for the serious but humorous confrontation between Cecil and Randolph as each man acts out his inherited and acquired views of civilization and of the relationship between man and woman. Lee notes that the mature Cecil, unlike Randolph, expects her to concede to his wishes, but that the experienced Randolph can outscheme the more methodical and learned Englishman. Nevertheless, she chooses marriage to Cecil because of his ability to excite her romantic imagination, and with her eyes open to the circumstantial causes of the differences between English and American points of view on marriage.

In Book II, the "grey imposing Fact" of English views affects Lee's expectations of marital happiness more than Cecil's. Though she adapts easily to English upper-class society, she becomes dissatisfied with her role as second self to Cecil's ambitions, and yearns for a return to her old ways. When a new financial threat to the continuity of Maundrell Abbey arises, Lee ironically submits to the traditional supportive view of the woman by employing her American wealth to keep the Abbey from falling into a scheming commoner's hands. The compromise between the stolid English husband and the independent, willful

American wife to maintain their link of two civilizations is worked out by a dramatic coincidence of their views.

In *American Wives and English Husbands,* Gertrude Atherton uses American and English characters in each other's environments, views a single psychological conflict, contrasts characters and scenes in the two books, and selects intensely dramatic scenes to objectify the essentially inner struggle of her heroine to shape her individuality. Some of these techniques suggest the influence of James's use of the international theme. Several issues underlie the action: the discrepancy between an American girl's upbringing and her actual destiny, the desire of women to be admired by men for their intellect as well as their physical charm and to be accepted as companions in marriage with independent interests of their own, and the cooperation rather than separation of husband and wife in achieving a happy marriage. As in *Patience Sparhawk,* the author employs an abrupt ending, the fashion of some contemporary novelists who wanted to suggest a problem of life or character.[7]

Mrs. Atherton's characterization of Lee and Cecil and her comparison of English and American views of the relation of the sexes carry "a vein of kindly satire."[8] Her resolution of their different views of the marital relationship might have reflected her recognition of the contradictory attitudes toward education of American girls and women and her concern for the rising divorce rate in America at the turn of the century.[9] Middle- and upper-class American girls like Lee were raised to be individuals and then expected to submerge their individualities in marriage. Randolph, with his good-humored praise of Lee's beauty and his acquiescence to her wishes, represents a type of American husband that contrasts sharply with Cecil's expectation that his wife will adapt herself to him and be responsible not only for her own happiness but also for his. After three years of marriage, Lee feels totally estranged from herself as well as from Cecil. Another satiric contrast in the novel involves an Englishman's accepting an American woman's money to save his ancestral home and remaining idle, against the narrator's claim that an American in such a circumstance would make a pretense at working after accepting the money. These satiric thrusts show Mrs. Atherton's awareness of her English readers and their foibles.

In presenting the discrepancies between the views of marriage based on love and money and held by the old and new civilizations, Mrs. Atherton carefully distributes her satire of English and American customs and attitudes. As a result, she chooses to develop Lee and Cecil's consciousness of their similarities, and their capacity to adapt to their changing needs in order to live as happy, fulfilled human beings. She dramatizes the tragic dissolution of the expedient marriage of Cecil's father, which is based on the need for money; hence she shows its logical end, and substitutes for it a different idea of marriage founded on fulfillment attained by each spouse's adaptiveness and acceptance of personal and societal obligations.

In this tragic subplot, Mrs. Atherton effectively portrays the earlier English-American romance, that of Cecil's father and step-mother, Emmy, a former resident of Chicago—the city that for Mrs. Atherton represented vulgarity and social power based on money. Emmy is discovered to have put the Abbey in jeopardy by borrowing funds to support it from a confidence man. This subplot provides both a contrast of American wives and English setting and a different angle of vision on Anglo-American civilization, and also produces the tragic climax and denouement. Cecil's father reveals to Lee that the necessity to preserve his old-world honor demands his suicide, and Lee submerges her new-world individuality in order to perpetuate that kind of honor through her continued support of Cecil Maundrell.

Mrs. Atherton employs a restrained style of narration and dialogue to relate objectively her American and English characters' ability to adapt to each other. She evokes the sense of both California's youthful lightness in the characterization of Lee and its primeval age in the image of the redwoods, and she contrasts this duality with the historic English beechwoods and monuments such as the Abbey. The matter-of-factness of the title and Mrs. Atherton's having written the novel at a publisher's request rather than as a spontaneous outpouring of her fictional tract result in a strong compound of romance and realism that convincingly illuminates the details of Cecil and Lee's adjustment of their personalities to each other and to their common pursuit of happiness. At the end of the novel, when Lee must inform Cecil of his father's suicide, she quietly considers the significance of the survival of generations of Maundrells despite the ancient abbot's curse on the family, and she, the contemporary generation, feels a mystical union with time and willfully submerges her California individuality for the sake of the continuity of the race and civilization.

IV   Ancestors: "Inner Landscapes" and "Nature's Currents"

Ancestors, Gertrude Atherton's longest novel (709 pages), in 1907 brought together and crystallized the most significant elements of her California story-chronicle and of her international theme. It covers a three year period—1904 in Britain and 1905 and 1906 in California—and envisions an opportunity for the British and American ideas of government to be joined in an extension of Western civilization on American soil. The novel focuses on the initiation stories of two self-conflicted characters: John Elton Gwynne, an American-born English aristocrat, and Isabel Otis, an independent California woman. The dilemmas of these characters embody several paradoxical aspects of the human condition in Western civilization that Mrs. Atherton had not successfully dramatized in her previous novels. Here the characterizations present from different angles new relationships between heredity and environment, between work and idleness, between liberty and license, and between love and happiness. In this novel, a man and a woman interact with a city and a state that like them are living organisms, attempting to discover an identity and a relation to nature. Mrs. Atherton made an epic attempt to connect in a new way the "inner landscapes" of a type of man and of woman to "nature's currents" and to civilization (pp. 525, 704).

In three parts, titled "1904," "1905," and "1906" respectively, Ancestors tells the story of the "affinity" of John Elton Gwynne, a Virginia-born Englishman, and his California-born third cousin, Isabel Otis. On the surface it is a romance. Underneath, it is a psychologically realistic story of two characters, battling against their inherited social duties in order to fulfill their inner desires for their own kind of purposeful life. The ongoing argument about the primary influence of heredity or environment on an individual becomes in this novel a balancing act deliberately undertaken by the major characters.

Gwynne is an English aristocrat with an indifferent and dominant personality because he is secure in his given duty to serve in the House of Lords; however, his Celtic blood, a "tiniest feminine drop" (p. 398), differentiates him from the usual type and encourages his rebellious desire to be a "genuine fighter," a "true liberal" in the House of Parliament. Ultimately he becomes "plain Jack Gwynne" in California. Isabel Otis is endowed with intellect, will, and inherited wealth that give her the liberty to discover and to follow her own conception of herself; however, attempting to find an appropriate substitute for the traditional woman's love and happiness in marriage, and to combine tradition and her own talent creates for her a double conflict between self and society. As third cousins, Jack and Isabel share two rebellious ancestors who were active at the same time, one in the West—Don Jose Arguëllo, Spanish commandante of the Presidio—and the other in the Northeast—Sam Adams—in the formation of the United States. Their common ancestral line and birthplace awaken in Jack and Isabel a desire to escape the complacency and ennui that can result from one's unthinking obedience to inherited beliefs and roles. Once they perceive a common goal in becoming leaders in San Francisco and California, they can conceive a different "affinity" between man and woman and a new base for civilization.

Gwynne grows up in the milieu of the upper class of Britain, and serves his country in the Boer War and in Parliament, although his real sympathies coincide with the concerns of the working man rather than with those of the Conservatives in Parliament. (In these details are resemblances to the career of Lord Randolph Churchill.) After falling in love with Julia Kaye, an Englishman's widow originally from Chicago, and ambitious for power in England through marriage, and after having won a difficult election as a Liberal, Gwynne at thirty years of age appears to have achieved a plan for his life. The sudden death of his uncle, who held the seat in Parliament, causes a crisis in this plan. If Gwynne occupies the hereditary seat, he must sacrifice his Liberal beliefs and his conviction that the monarchy must be reformed. If he refuses the seat, he sacrifices his own inherited identity and loses the woman that he thinks he loves.

During this crisis, narrated in Part I, Isabel Otis is visiting at Gwynne's ancestral estate, and she challenges him to take up his American birthright and to build a political career out of his own talent as plain Jack Gwynne in the United States. Accepting the challenge, Gwynne in Part II begins a conscious examination of his "undercurrent" self (p. 399) and of the new social and political milieu he has consciously chosen. Though frequently desiring to return to his fame and opportunity as Elton Gwynne in England, he discovers that his escape from his inherited identity and purpose has allowed him to experience a confrontation with nature and civilization that in England would have been denied to him. He renews his zest for living by becoming a naturalized American citizen and trying to see people as human beings without classifying them by external appearance or circumstances of birth. He learns to shed his own aristocratic shell so that he can democratically represent the constituents that he wishes to serve eventually in the United States Senate. The transformation of an already formed and successful Elton Gwynne to a self-made Jack Gwynne suggests that Mrs. Atherton observed certain social and cultural restrictions on man's as well as on woman's opportunities to unite the private self with inherited public expectations.

Isabel Otis has the typical upbringing of an upper middle-class woman, and cares for her alcoholic lawyer-father until his death liberates her from traditional womanly duties. Isabel considers herself independent of this tradition because she enjoys intellectual solitude and successfully manages the chicken ranch north of San Francisco which she has inherited. She also considers herself liberated because she has avoided the "tyranny of love" that she believes narrows a woman's interests and warps the imagination. While attempting to prove that she is freed from the game of life that is a sham, a "fool's paradise," Isabel searches for a different purpose and fantasizes a life of the imagination as a replacement for tyrannous passion. Hence Jack Gwynne's crisis provides her with a new and "clearly defined intention" to be a factor in his political career in California without the necessity to love or to marry him.

Throughout the first two parts of the novel, Isabel and Jack work toward a social role for themselves, especially in San Francisco, a city needing social and political leadership in those corrupt years. They are impersonal toward each other, acting as people learning to respect liberty in interpersonal relationships. Their concept of personal liberty is expressed by an indifference that is intended to prevent their "taking a liberty" with each other or someone else's "taking a liberty" with them. Each is fearful of being dominated by the other, yet both want and enjoy the intellectual and passionate companionship that their types of characters promise. Isabel much longer resists the possibility of love and marriage because of her sense of the confinement of domesticity and her disbelief in the possibilities of happiness through marriage. After perverse misunderstandings and willful battles, however, she and Jack finally recognize their need for each other, and Isabel agrees to marriage only when they both believe that they can have a meaningful life together.

The morning after their declaration of love, the earthquake of 1906 strikes, unselectively purging with fire the good and the corrupt. Their love and the accident of nature appear to symbolize the possibility of a new civilization being built by a vigilant cooperation of all human beings and by a recognition of a liberating companionship in the relationship of the sexes. "Inner landscapes" and "nature's currents" and civilization become one.

In the characterization of Jack Gwynne and of Isabel Otis, Gertrude Atherton again deals with the Western custom of romantic love that camouflages affinity—the instinct of the race to perpetuate itself. In their shared experience, Jack and Isabel act out the author's plan for frustrating the "tyrannical schemes of nature" to rush young people into marriage; they choose each other with their "highly developed egos" rather than with their "nervous systems." Shortly after *Ancestors* was published (it eventually ranked third on the best-sellers list in 1907), Mrs. Atherton explained how the novel deals with affinity:

The hero and the heroine were a long time "falling in love," and when they finally did, it was with their eyes open, after they, as well as the reader, had been brought to see that they were admirably fitted to assist each other in the eternal battle with life. There was no sense of "affinity," no falling in love at first sight; it was emphasized that in other circumstances they would not have suited each other at all. . . . But in the peculiar conditions that arose, their life companionship became as sure as fate, and they had an opportunity to accomplish something together, which is more than can be said of most married couples. No doubt, also, they would be happier than most, not only in this accomplishment, but because as individuals, highly developed, they must find each other more interesting than the average human being, and grow persistently.[10]

Thus Isabel Otis and Jack Gwynne stand as Mrs. Atherton's most highly developed exemplars of a new woman and a new man.

Well-drawn minor characters as self-conscious and analytical

as Jack and Isabel serve to expand Mrs. Atherton's observation of
the effect of the traditional womanhood against which Isabel
rebels. Among traditional Englishwomen, Julia Kaye and Flora
Thangue, the latter a Jamesian *ficelle*, are respectively a type
who seeks power that is available to a woman only through
marriage, and a type prevented from marriage by familial duty
who substitutes various friendships with titled and wealthy
women as her life purpose. The reader is repelled by Julia and
sympathetic toward Flora. The characterization of Lady Victoria
Gwynne, Jack's widowed mother, still possessing vitality and
beauty at fifty, remarkably focuses the dilemma of woman—how
to live with zest and self-fulfillment before and after racial and
maternal duties have been accomplished. Lady Victoria must
replace her material concern for her mature son with another
affectional connection or suffer a debilitating ennui that results
from her having outlived youthful beauty and the opportunity to
use her intellectual ability. Her liberty to choose new associa-
tions is far greater in aristocratic England than in America,
especially in provincial San Francisco, where certain kinds of
liaisons would be censored as "license" (p. 541).

Annabel Colton, submerged in domesticity and children;
middle-class Mrs. Hofer, whose marriage into wealth develops
her capacity to manage happily a husband, several children, and
an active position in San Francisco Society; and Anne Montgomery, who sentimentally allows her family's attitude about a
"woman who did things" (p. 501) to prevent her from becoming a
concert musician—all are American types who are affected by
the traditional view of woman. Along with Isabel, despite her
ideal of the independent woman, all of these characters find
their only real and acceptable destiny defined by their
relationship with other human beings. Isabel Otis and Mrs.
Atherton seem to accept this fact of nature with reluctance.

Other succinctly portrayed characters hone Jack Gwynne's
aristocratic habits to the democratic necessities of political
action. The cynical young Democratic politician, Tom Colton,
rising on the coattails of labor; Republican Judge Leslie, too
"dead straight" to play politics; Larkin T. Boutts, a businessman
fearful of the extension of ownership of land to Japanese and
other immigrants; and Lyster Stone, Bohemian artist, who
introduces Jack to the underside of San Francisco—all instruct
the new American in the elements of local American politics and

manners. Jack learns how to talk frankly about political positions with the amoral Colton, who will become his chief opponent for public office, by declaring: "Nothing degrades human nature nor retards civilization so much as politics gone altogether wrong. . . . The moment I am in power I shall devote my energies to pulling you and your like down and out" (p. 635).

Mrs. Atherton effectively evokes the *genius loci* of San Francisco. The city, its ancestors, and the effect it has on its various types of inhabitants make it a significant romantic character as well as a realistic milieu in Parts II and III of the novel. Details of the beauty of San Francisco, its careless, turbulent history, its Southern social set of the 1860s and 1870s, the financial booms and busts of the 1880s, the decade of decent, honorable government in the 1890s are woven in and out of the narrative like another wayward and individualistic character attempting to find its identity. Characters from Mrs. Atherton's earlier San Francisco novels form a social backdrop against which can be viewed Isabel and Jack's current adventure in balancing heredity and environment. At the same time, the city serves as the testing ground for their campaign to launch Jack's new political career, and the city's terrible destruction in 1906 inspires both of them with the spirit of pioneering that had prevailed in the 1850s and which they hope will allow San Francisco to be consciously built this time by the many kinds of people who inhabit it.

Readers of *Ancestors* may object to the fullness of Mrs. Atherton's treatment of her themes. One reviewer claimed that her insertion of political customs and conversations and the nonessential intrusions of the real world into the novel were a test of the author as a Realist.[11] Mrs. Atherton dared to imagine that such a sweeping change of social and cultural attitudes could be envisioned and acted upon by one man and one woman in three years. She sacrificed certain advantages of narrative brevity for the sake of greater fidelity to all of the pertinent aspects of her theme as she saw it. Hence, despite the more than seven hundred pages of the novel, she achieves an economy of narrative and dramatic structure by designing Part I, 1904, to evoke the character and milieu of John Elton Gwynne; Part II, 1905, the longest section, to present Isabel Otis on her home ground and in her intention to make an American politician of Jack Gwynne and to free him from maternal influence; and Part

III, 1906, to set the stage for Jack and Isabel, as representative
Americans, to discover a common goal in the rebuilding of a
civilization.

Gertrude Atherton focuses her epic even more sharply by
urging that San Francisco and California stand for all of the
United States in the first decade of the twentieth century. Hence
the corruption of San Francisco, like that of New York City
earlier, and the capital-labor problems with immigrant workers
in California may represent nationwide issues such as graft and
antitrust action. In this concentrated American milieu, the
transplanted Englishman, who declares that every American is
an "unhatched Englishman," can learn how Americans
"reformed" the English monarchy.

In *Ancestors*, Mrs. Atherton shows greater awareness of
fictional techniques than she had before. Her use of Flora
Thangue as a *ficelle* as well as a character-chorus, who is more
interested in others than in herself, condenses much of the
exposition necessary in Part I. And Mrs. Atherton's omniscient
narrator reveals the inner perturbations of Jack and Isabel as
well as describes the outer evidence of internal upheavals of
human beings and nature. Throughout her comparison of English
and American mores and character, the novelist with both wit
and humor praises and chastises her new man and new woman in
the "fool's paradise" that they expect to rebuild.

V *California Potboilers*

In the six other books utilizing California material and
published in the decade before and after the turn of the century,
Gertrude Atherton exercised her sense of connecting the theme
and the sale of her works to current circumstances in the real
world. In the same year as *The Californians* and *American Wives
and English Husbands* appeared *The Valiant Runaways* (1898).
It is an adventure story for boys, concerned with the early
Spanish-Mexican attempt to civilize California, and is a minor
display of Mrs. Atherton's ironic and vigorous narrative method,
as the boys run away from their homes to escape conscription
into the army but actually run right into battle.

The next year appeared *A Daughter of the Vine* (1899),
written near Haworth, the home of the Brontës, while the author
awaited publication of *Patience Sparhawk*. This novel is a revised

version of her first published story of 1883, concerning the alcoholic demise of a member of a prominent San Francisco family. The author unsuccessfully attempts to establish a connection of the Gordon family of San Francisco with Branwell Brontë. Although the morbid theme of inherited alcoholism remains dominant in the novel, Mrs. Atherton adds an ironic comparison of the gloomy and ancient English atmosphere by placing the "tragedy" in California, a "land of such exultant beauty" that it lends itself not at all to anything deeper than the "picturesque crimes of desperadoes" (pp. 101 - 102).

In *The Splendid Idle Forties* (1902), Mrs. Atherton added several stories of early California to a collection that had been published without much critical attention in 1894 under the title *Before the Gringo Came.* Apparently she intended to capitalize on the high acclaim and popularity of her dramatized biography of Alexander Hamilton, *The Conqueror* (1902). The publication of another collection of short stories, *The Bell in the Fog* (1905), dedicated to Henry James, coincided with James's first visit in twenty years to the United States and his first to California. Only two of the stories contain California themes. Neither collection added to her development as a writer.

The Traveling Thirds (1905) is a light romance in Spain between Catalina Shore, a California woman with mixed Indian and New England blood, and an Englishman. Catalina's New England uncle, Mr. Moulton, with whom she travels, bears a curious resemblance to William Dean Howells. However, the novel characterizes him rather gently in contrast to Mrs. Atherton's lambasting of Howells in literary periodicals and newspaper articles between 1904 and 1908 as the cause of the dull and unimaginative American literature. *Rezánov* (1906), relating a nearly forgotten event in San Francisco's history in 1806, appeared several months after the devastation of the Bay area by the earthquake of 1906. The conventional love story involving Mrs. Atherton's types of uncommon lovers, as in *The Doomswoman*—in this case, a Russian explorer and a daughter of the Spanish commander of Monterey—does not breathe life into the characters, but the atmospheric charm of California is evoked credibly.

CHAPTER 4

Social History as Fiction: The Interaction of Personality and Environment

A S a "correct" historian, delineating the places, circumstances and types of people of her times, Gertrude Atherton went beyond her characterization of a California woman. Between 1900 and 1915, she chose several actual people and groups of people in certain circumstances as her inspiration for figures in novels. Five such novels maintained the high standards of the best of her California series, while others appeared to be published to take advantage of her growing literary reputation. Senator Eugene Hale of Maine, a Republican Senator from 1881 to 1911, analytical in temperament and opposed to war with Spain in 1898, served as the model for the sixty-year-old statesman and lover in *Senator North* (1900). In *The Conqueror* (1902), Alexander Hamilton played himself in Mrs. Atherton's invention of a biography utilizing the methods of fiction. Three opera singers, active in Munich in the early 1900s, inspired the characterization of the novelist's favorite woman character, Margarethe Styr, in her favorite novel, *Tower of Ivory* (1910) — in which Ludwig II of Bavaria played himself. Several of Mrs. Atherton's friends in London rather than the major suffragists of London were catalysts for characters in *Julia France and Her Times* (1912), the one novel that the author reported that she wrote less for her own pleasure and more as an obligation to explore the social and political aspects of her sex.[1] The business of mining and the social life among the inhabitants of Butte, Montana, where Mrs. Atherton lived briefly, provide a different Western background and new types of characters in *Perch of the Devil* (1914), a novel of a small town that antedated Sinclair Lewis's *Main Street* by six years.

I   Senator North: *"To Live Now . . .
in the Midst of Current History"*

Senator North (1900) narrates the story of the desire of
Southern, aristocratic Betty Madison to "live now . . . to be in the
midst of current history" at the end of the nineteenth century by
going into politics in Washington. Through family friends and
through the social custom of "calling" and "days," Betty becomes
acquainted with several senators, including Robert Burleigh of a
midwestern state and Senator North of Maine, both of whom
admire her beauty and intellect and urge her to have a salon
where the best minds of the capital can discuss the issues of the
times. Her immediate success in this form of politics and her
idealized friendship with Senator North are interrupted by the
arrival of a half-sister, heretofore unknown to her: Harriet
Madison is the daughter of an octoroon mistress of Betty's father.
Senator North advises Betty to accept Harriet into her home, and
Betty provides Harriet with a portion of her father's estate and
instructs her in appropriate social behavior.

In the Adirondacks for the summer, Betty Madison ponders
her growing love for Senator North, complicated by the fact of
his invalid wife, and her feelings for Senator Burleigh, who has
proposed marriage. Harriet and Jack Emory, Betty's cousin with
staunch Southern ideas, fall in love and secretly marry without
Jack's knowing of Harriet's background. After Harriet finally
confesses her parentage to Jack, he takes his life and Harriet
drowns herself. Shaken by her inability to alter the circumstances that caused the suicides, Betty returns to Washington.
There the war fever rises over the incident of the *Maine*, and war
is declared in spite of Senator North's attempt quietly to
persuade votes against it while publicly he is obliged to support
the Republican president's decision to declare war. Once again
circumstances both hinder and aid Betty's desired fate: she is
unable to support publicly Senator North's antiwar arguments or
to comfort him when his antiwar efforts are defeated, but the
death of his wife opens the possibility of their marriage and a
political life together.

The two romances compose Mrs. Atherton's "fable" of
American politics and Washington personalities in this novel that
a London friend suggested that she write for an English
audience.[2] In writing *American Wives and English Husbands*, the

author had learned that readers resist a novel with a title that
suggests a series of essays on some topic of interest. Hence the
"fable" of idealistic love camouflages her realistic observations
of the maneuverings for position and power by aristocrats,
democrats, populists, and lobbyists in the social and political
milieu of the nation's capital; her "fable" of love, made tragic
because inherited social attitudes and belief in the transmission
of certain racial characteristics affect future generations, is
carried to its logical and unsentimental conclusion. The secondary romance, furthermore, serves as an aid to Betty's re-
evaluation of her inherited idea of racial relations, the propriety
of amorous liaisons for the sake of power or personal enhance-
ment, and the antagonism of her will and love. When Betty
chooses to idealize Senator North rather than to succumb to a
love affair, the American author ironically comments for her
English audience on the well-known liberties of the English
upper class. Ultimately, the effect of individual and national
attitudes in respect to superior and inferior races is satirically
joined in the tragic outcome of Jack and Harriet's love and in a
war sentimentally undertaken in behalf of a supposedly
downtrodden nation.

Mrs. Atherton's characterizations are ironic portrayals of
personalities in Washington, a city which she describes as a
"democracy with a kernel of the most exclusive aristocracy"
(p. 26), and they subtly explore the effect of environment on
these personalities and their inherited notions. All the lovers
except Harriet Madison embody Mrs. Atherton's typical
aristocratic and idealized personality, though Senator North and
Betty Madison are individualized as they interact with people of
different political attitudes and social levels. Jack Emory, Sally
Carter, and Mrs. Madison, Betty's mother, represent the
traditional Southern position on social relationships among
people of different classes and races, and among these only Mrs.
Madison eventually exhibits some acceptance of politicians as
her social equals.

While Harriet's regression in the Adirondacks to Negro hymn-
singing reflects the contemporary belief in inherited behavior,
through exposure to literature and the French language and
through association with the Madisons she develops a semblance
of the desirable aloofness of the well-born. Similarly, Betty's
inherited antipathy toward the Negro becomes mixed with pity

for her half-sister, whom she comes to understand as a "victim of one of the vices of civilization and men that persisted to its logical climax" (p. 260). The lower-class people and tourists, who consider that Washington belongs to them, are depicted not only for the humor of their observations of political behavior but also for revealing the complex interaction of all kinds of people in a representative form of government. Betty discharges the gossiping, vain, and moralistic housekeeper, Miss Trumbull, who uncovers the secret marriage of Jack and Harriet. Later Betty has to alter her relationship with Miss Trumbull, who, having married a midwestern Congressman, attends the same public and social functions Betty does.

In the characterization of Senator North, Mrs. Atherton paid tribute to the role of a United States senator, his constitutional responsibilities, and his obligation, like that of the aristocrat's *noblesse oblige*, to decide for the "people to whose destiny he is a constituted guardian and defender" rather than for his own interests. Her epigraph to *Senator North* excerpted this senatorial ideal from a memorial address before the Senate in 1866 by William Pitt Fessenden, a senator of Maine, who, like Senator Hale and Alexander Hamilton, exemplified Mrs. Atherton's ideal of honest, conservative statesmanship and personal integrity. Senator North's loyal public defense of President McKinley's declaration of war in 1898 while privately decrying it echoes the historical record of Senator Hale. After his personal defeat on the issue of war, Senator North dreams that Hamilton understood his disappointment in the unthinking emotionalism of Americans and a Senate that thrust aside the nation's ideals and plunged it into war (pp. 344 - 50).

In addition, the author creates in Senator North a type of man especially attractive as a mentor and lover of her self-centered and self-conflicted heroine. A remarkable departure from the typical fictional American hero, North at sixty possesses intellectual and sexual energy that he devotes to marital and senatorial duties and to a woman half his age who demands his attention. His socially correct behavior toward Betty and his approval of her confused search for a fitting public role offset some inconsistencies in his characterization.

A typical heroine, Betty Madison is a Virginia-born "independent intellect caught and tangled in a fishnet of traditions" and in a conflict between curiosity and ennui in modern Washington.

Her attempt to find happiness and to participate in political life is largely but very seriously a mental one (p. 174), because of her continual self-analysis and her inclination toward a passionate and spiritual idealization of the relationship between man and woman. Betty faces two needs: to balance her aristocratic views with those of the democratic process and to control willfully her capacity for love and her imaginative retreat from living. The first she is able to rationalize through observing politics at work from the Senate Gallery, through social activities and through long conversations with Senator North. The second, however, causes her romantic suffering, because she cannot will the end of her love of Senator North or accept the proposal of the midwestern Burleigh.

These two needs generate the dramatic scenes and interior monologues that show her confused thinking and self-conflict. Although Betty intellectually approves the Negro minister's admonishment to his congregation to improve their minds and characters (p. 14), emotionally she accepts the typical Southern view of the Negro, held by her cousin Jack, that it is impossible to undo the harm already done. As the tragedy of Jack and Harriet logically results from this viewpoint, Betty is led to connect it with the Senate's decision to support the Cubans' desire for freedom from Spain, even as she supports the aristocratic, conservative position of Senator North and of Spain. Watching the Senate vote for a war against Spain that would "alter forever the position of the United States in the family of nations," Betty Madison is affected so powerfully that her "ego seemed dead" and she is conscious only of "looking down upon history" and of seeing the "Senate for the time . . . a unit" (pp. 333 - 34). Later, blindly raging at social circumstance, which prevents her from comforting Senator North in his defeat, she again transcends her self-consciousness by deciding to protect his and the nation's future against her present need to share his experience (p. 340). The recording of Betty's attempt to overcome self-consciousness is a fictional enactment of the effort of a certain type of woman to be taken seriously.

Senator North tests Mrs. Atherton's aim to be a "correct historian" of her times. In several months she explored the nation's capital from the "cave people"—old Washingtonians— to the "dames of Plutocracy," and from the Senate Gallery to private conversations with legislators and lobbyists.[3] She describes White House receptions, private parties, and senatorial actions with an authentic sense of place and costume. Placing her fiction in history, she credibly links incidents involving her characters with several of the critical issues before the Senate, such as the tariff bill of President McKinley, the silver question, the arbitration treaty with Great Britain, and especially the public hysteria, abetted by the press, that resulted from the sinking of the *Maine* and that led to the declaration of war against Spain. Mrs. Atherton's ironic view of "the business of Society," of old-fashioned and dreamy Southern attitudes that lacked "modern grip" (p. 212), and of woman's "desperate battle with Circumstance" (p. 251) touches on some causes of unrest in the decade that Larzer Ziff has called "the lost generation."[4]

The three-part structure of *Senator North* shows the author increasing her control of the relationships among character, action, setting, and tone. The action takes place in Washington in Parts I and III and in the Adirondacks in Part II. Washington represents the present circumstances of the nation and of certain individuals that are based upon the attitudes and actions of an earlier stage—the primitive nature of mankind associated with the Adirondacks—and carried to their logical conclusion. Hence the tragedy, resulting from a racial attitude and occurring in the Adirondacks, establishes a comparison with the Spanish-Cuban situation and the modern American action upon it. Looking back on the personal tragedy, Betty Madison muses—

I had engaged in a conflict with the unseen Forces of life and had been conquered . . . had been obliged to stand by and see these forces work their will upon a helpless being, who carried in solution the vices of civilizations and men persisting to their logical climax, almost demanding aloud the sacrifice of the victim to death that this portion of themselves might be buried with her . . . nothing else could have given her so clear a realization of the eternal persistence of all acts, of the sequential symmetrical links that forge in the great chain of Circumstance. (pp. 260 - 61)

In answer to the critical objection that the theme of miscegenation was disconnected and was treated with "cruel brutality," Mrs. Atherton wrote in a letter to the *New York Times* that the tragedy as well as the relationship of Senator North and Betty Madison were logical conclusions of long-held beliefs.[5]

II   The Conqueror: *"To Give the Man"*

The Conqueror, Being the True and Romantic Story of Alexander Hamilton (1902) is the only book by Gertrude Atherton with a man as the protagonist. It focuses attention on the social and political ascent of Alexander Hamilton from his relatively obscure youth in the West Indies to his actions in his adopted country from 1772 to 1804, and it describes the actual persons who with Hamilton were involved in the formation of a government of a diverse people. As a new form of biography utilizing the methods of fiction, *The Conqueror* was designed "to give the man" as well as the statesman and to be read at a time when biography was attracting few readers.[6] The novel also added a different dimension to the historical novel because of its narration of historical incidents and people who were observed as much in their social interactions as in their political significance.

The Conqueror is placed in the West Indies, where Alexander Hamilton was born, and in the colonies and states of North America in the last half of the eighteenth century. The circumstances of the common-law marriage of Hamilton's parents, his birth on Nevis in 1757, the death of his mother, his success as head of a counting house at the age of fourteen, and his departure for New York for his education are related in the first fourth of the book. These pages romanticize the few facts of Hamilton's first fifteen years and of the social history of the British West Indies, laying the basis for the declaration of Hamilton's instructor, Hugh Knox, that his pupil is an aristocrat in body and brain (p. 117). The remainder of the book recounts the thoughts and actions and the personal and social sides of Hamilton the man, and delineates his associations with George Washington, John Adams, Thomas Jefferson, James Madison, and Aaron Burr, and with his family and paramours. The fiction comprises the author's imagining the intimate facets of Hamilton's life, such as the boyish abandon in his domestic life; the motives of the well-known characters; the conversations between public figures on public occasions and in the privacy of boudoirs; the emotions swirling around objective historical fact; and the details of costuming and social affairs that knit together social and political fact (pp. 341, 384-85).

In the context of her purpose of giving Hamilton back to the American people as a hero and a man, Gertrude Atherton's characterization of the major historical personages appears to differ from the usual perception of them. Basic to her presentation is the conflict between the aristocratic statesman and the democratic individualist. George Washington, John Adams, and Hamilton represent the statesman-aristocrat; Thomas Jefferson, James Madison, and Aaron Burr, the emerging self-interested and expedient politician (p. 468). She emphasizes Washington's paternal love of Hamilton and reliance on him for military leadership, for writing his correspondence, and even for composing his Farewell Address (p. 438). In Mrs. Atherton's eyes, Washington and Hamilton decide matters for the good of the country rather than as a satisfaction of their egos. John Adams, described as a "grim old Puritan," irascible, jealous, and ambitious, but well dressed even though a farmer by birth, is observed to be as aristocratic in his tastes as Washington and Hamilton. Pursuing this distinction, the author portrays Jefferson as a farmer, torn between his plebeian father and aristocratic mother, and opposing Hamilton's federalist notion of government by a select group of leaders, that Jefferson fears will endanger a democracy of self-governed men. Likewise, the Virginia triumvirate of Madison, Jefferson, and Monroe is envisioned as waiting to rescue the new federalist government from its tottering condition. Aaron Burr, the grandsire of Tammany Hall and the ultimate nemesis of Hamilton, is made an opponent worthy of Hamilton despite his corrupt and treasonable dealings with the French, his political division of New York, and his actions in regard to the Manhattan Bank.

Important in all of Mrs. Atherton's characterizations of the historical figures are the series of assaults against Hamilton that his opponents made and the statesmanlike responses that Hamilton returned in speeches, pamphlets, and political action, all of which upheld his federalist point of view.

In portraying the historical women, Mrs. Atherton emphasized their capacity for mental acumen and ability to mature. Through careful search of court and church records on several islands in the British West Indies, she attempted to verify the aristocratic origins of Rachel Levine, Hamilton's mother, whom she describes as a beautiful, intellectual woman and whom Hamilton remembered after her death in the sound of golden bells. Betsy Schuyler, Hamilton's wife, at first is a typical upper-class spouse and mother, but she becomes a subtle coquette and intellectual companion of Hamilton when his affair with Mrs. Croix develops into a serious issue between them. The characterization of Mrs. Croix declines from an emphasis on her beauty, intellect, and passion to a stress on her cunning and revenge when Hamilton chooses fidelity to Betsy over a continuing intrigue with his paramour. The preferences of costume and manner of entertainment of Martha Washington, Abigail Adams, Mrs. Croix, and the men embellish the novel's fabric of political issues and intrigue.

In her determination that biography ought to differ from the old form and ought to "give the man" in order to be more readable, Mrs. Atherton employs "the form of life ... writing ... as if I had stood beside Hamilton throughout his life."[7] In imagining a way of walking beside him, she avoids a first-person contemporary narrator and utilizes her usual omniscient one, who frequently speaks to her current audience to make comparisons between Hamilton's day and the first years of the twentieth century. This device allows the narrator to comment on a series of points of interest to Mrs. Atherton: attitudes toward the civil and natural rights of women as well as of men (pp. 42, 129); the feeble bourgeois spirit of 1902 as compared to the independent and romantic temper of the late eighteenth century (p. 169); the federal constitution proposed by Hamilton and the one ratified; the psychology of social interaction; the ignoble sides of the major historical figures and of Hamilton as found in their biographies. The "walking" narrator also paces the telling of Hamilton's life by telescoping certain periods in order to develop the next climax in his career and by discarding those wearisome details of living that readers turn to books to forget. In spite of the narrator's partisanship toward Hamilton, the author declared that she might idolize Hamilton, but she did not idealize him.[8]

What is the nature of *The Conqueror?* It contains historical fact gathered from historical documents and biographies of the historical characters; from conversations with descendants of Hamilton's family; and from details of social history gleaned from research *in situ.* And it is a realistic romance of an extraordinary British citizen who contributed much to his adopted country. In a new edition of *The Conqueror* in 1916, Mrs. Atherton added the subtitle *A Dramatized Biography of Alexander Hamilton,* probably because she considered a character novel a dramatized biography.[9] In 1930, Fred Lewis Pattee acknowledged *The Conqueror* to be a pioneer work in what was later known as the Maurois school of biographical fiction.[10] In answering controversial responses of readers and critics to *The Conqueror,* the author strongly supported her novelistic treatment of historical matter. In the introduction to her edition of Hamilton's letters—*A Few of Hamilton's Letters* (1903)—she claimed that she exhibited Hamilton's faults and weaknesses with "considerable pleasure," for no man can be "great or lovable without them."

III   Tower of Ivory: *"An Almost Perfect Experience"*

Tower of Ivory (1910) is an anti-romance dealing with the lives of two aloof characters, Margarethe Styr and John Ordham, who prefer the ego's ivory tower of sensations to the mundane world's matrimony. Styr, born Margaret Hill to immigrant workers in the coal fields in America, rises from her early life as a professional courtesan and actress to become a protégé of King Ludwig II of Bavaria because of her unique interpretation of Wagnerian opera. The Englishman Ordham, a "flower" of the British aristocratic system, anticipating a coronet and becoming a diplomat, scarcely knows his inner capacities and barely manages to fulfill the diplomatic accomplishments expected of him. Their first meeting at Ludwig's castle, Neuschwanstein, sets in motion their temperamental reactions to changes in their mental and emotional circumstances.

Styr and Ordham, twelve years younger than she, are immediately attracted to each other despite her preference for a solitary artistic life and his aristocratic reserve and passivity. Ordham's manner and indolence prompt Styr and several middle-aged and unattached women to act as "potters" of his destiny. Princess Nachmeister, the social leader of Munich, Lady Bridgminister, Ordham's mother, and American Mrs. Cutting plot to arrange his marriage either to an Englishwoman or to a wealthy "American princess," while Styr encourages his diplomatic studies. Yet at the time of his return to London to take his diplomatic examinations and in an ironic turn of expectations, Ordham and Styr in romantic Munich have found in each other a "mental marriage."

Ordham's family's indebtedness, the presence of the wealthy "American princess," Mabel Cutting, and his continuing passivity about his career apparently coalesce and produce his first experience of passion for a woman. Ordham's marriage to Mabel arouses Styr's "primitive instincts" of passion, buried long ago so that she could dedicate herself to her artistic career and prevent her from becoming interested in other people. Fearing that Ordham's society-centered marriage will undermine his dip-lomatic goal, she eventually writes to remind him of his career; and to prod him to some kind of action, she explains that, because of Ludwig's plight in Munich, she lacks a protector in the politics of the operatic world.

This appeal, his disappointment in Mabel's lack of intellectual development, and his wife and mother's blocking of his diplomatic assignment on the Continent arouse an unexpectedly hard core in Ordham's personality, and he ruthlessly begins to take charge of his life. Ordham arranges a season of Wagnerian opera in London for Styr, and because of their proximity during this time, their "mental marriage" develops into love while his feeling for Mabel, now pregnant, steadily declines. Even Mabel's sudden death in childbirth does not deter Ordham from rushing immediately to claim Styr in Munich, where he finds her singing her renunciation of earthly marriage in the role of Brünhilde in the Hof House, empty save for Ludwig II. Foreseeing in a marriage to Ordham a sacrifice of her art and a lack of social acceptance in diplomatic circles because of her early pro-miscuous and theatrical life, Styr sings the role of Brünhilde as a fusion of the significance of Isolde and Brünhilde—a woman choosing pure passion and death. Then she plunges into the flames of Siegfried's bier and does not emerge. Her artistic renunciation merges with Mabel's death to catalyze the indolent Ordham to achieve success in diplomacy.

Tower of Ivory is set in the 1880s in London because of the prominence of the literary image of the "American princess" and of pending literary and theatrical changes that could accommo-date Ibsen, Wagner, and later Wilde; and it is also set in Munich during the same years in order to include Ludwig's passion for Wagner's new music and to portray a society where many different nationalities and levels of society could intermingle freely and pleasurably. For this setting Mrs. Atherton created several characters from types of people that she knew well during her residence in Munich in the early 1900s, a period that she considered "an almost perfect experience."[11] Styr exhibits characteristics of three of the novelist's friends, who were involved in this great period of Munich's operatic history— Maude Fay, the San Francisco-born lyric soprano, who sang the

Wagnerian roles of Elizabeth, Elsa, and Sieglinde; Marcia Van Dresser, a lyric soprano, who, like Styr, performed on the American stage; and Adenka Fassbender, a Bohemian-born dramatic soprano. Fassbender's golden voice and personality and her ability to create the complete illusion in opera led Mrs. Atherton to base her characterization of Styr primarily on this "risen Isolde and Brünhilde."[12] Moreover, in her friend John Lambton, who came to Munich to study German because his father had chosen a diplomatic career for him and who later became the Earl of Durham, Mrs. Atherton found a "highly interesting study" of an individual that revealed a whole class, and imitated him in John Ordham.

In the characterization of Ordham, Mrs. Atherton ironically examines the social man like Cecil Maundrell and Jack Gwynne, who heretofore in her fictional world had been a fair sample of all that civilization had accomplished and whose inheritance gave their lives a purpose which they eventually took charge of and fulfilled. Ordham's manners and indolent helplessness create a pleasant pattern of existence for him until his manipulation into marriage and his desire for Styr awaken both his latent obstinacy and his energy. Then he consciously uses good manners to put aside any obstacle in his desire for Styr, who in turn admires his "hardness" as "man epitomized" (p. 428), but who decides to die on the stage and to live on as the love of his heart.

Reversals in roles, images, and motives help to define the double life of the heroine and illustrate her development by reactions to other personalities and forces. Margarethe Styr, the American woman, plays Pygmalion to the Englishman Ordham. As a familiar fictional type—a woman with a past who is usually treated with disdain—Margaret Hill, by willing her sensuous past into high art, becomes admirable Margarethe Styr. This transformation creates for Styr a kind of "fool's paradise," because she believes that she can sublimate passion forever beneath an ideal existence in her tower apartment along the romantic Isar River. Her "ivory" composure, enhanced by ivory skin and luminous eyes, form the foundation for the contrasting and startling passion with which Styr interprets the Wagnerian heroines by divesting them of all their conventional interpretations. The "ivory" private life and the passionate artistic life, however, make Styr vulnerable to the temptation to influence a personality like that of Ordham.

Styr's double life also enables her to express artistically, in the

roles of Isolde and Brünhilde, an elemental problem of woman as
defined in Western civilization. In all the Wagnerian roles sung
by Styr are the traditional social roles of women—Isolde and
Sieglinde, the passionate, lawless heroines (p. 410); Elsa and
Elizabeth, respectively a spontaneous, naive lover and a virgin
who renounces her love to save her beloved; and Brünhilde, a
woman deprived of her status as a god and becoming woman to
be a pawn of kings and warriors. In Styr's final performance of
the Götterdämmerung, which she sings only for Ludwig and
Ordham, Ordham recognizes that she may be communicating to
him her decision to marry him or to remain with her art. More
importantly, Styr synthesizes the significant role of Isolde and
Brünhilde, which Wagner had separated. In this interpretation,
originating in a woman's view of existence, Styr sings the role of
Isolde with the composer's idea that passion has imprescriptible
rights, superior to all law and human judgment, provided it is
absolute, doomed, and willing to accept death as its sole refuge.
Styr adds to the role a woman's desire for a happy memory of the
joy of love before death comes. In singing Brünhilde previously,
Styr had portrayed "woman epitomized, arguing that all great
women had the ichor of the goddess in their veins, and that
primal woman was but the mother of a sex modified (sometimes)
but not remade" (p. 452). In this final performance, Styr synthesizes Isolde's passion and sacrifice of life, Elizabeth's virginal
sweetness and sacrifice of love, and Brünhilde's ecstatic
acceptance of her womanhood in order to give "the final
expression to the first love of woman" that is alloyed with the
knowledge of these conflicting elements in the human desire to
love and be loved and to be artist and social being. The synthesis
embodies Mrs. Atherton's vision of a whole woman. In a
Nietzschean-Wagnerian negation of the will to live, Styr
achieves redemption of her early immoral loves and a perfect
memory of the joy of a first real love. The characterization
creates a literary image of a whole and knowing woman.

The portrayal of three women, who like Ordham are
individualized products of a social system, illustrates Mrs.
Atherton's skill as a social historian who reveals the psychology
of their self-limited characters by linking them with cultural
elements. Lady Bridgminster is the mother of six sons, including
Ordham, who recalling that as a young girl she was painted by

Rossetti as the embodiment of Beatrice, judges that this early recognition contributed to his mother's "fatal desire to express [in her life] so much more than she could conceive" (p. 204). Nonetheless, under her aesthetically delicate appearance, Lady Bridgminster is hard and supple as a Toledo blade; without loss of purpose, she adapts to her reduced circumstances on the death of her husband. The wealthy and puritanical American wife, Mrs. Cutting, exemplifying the mutual neglect of spouses in the marriage of the leisured class, trains her idolized daughter to be an American beauty, and in her own way she loves her daughter's husband. On the other hand, Mabel, at first delighted to be admired as the Blessed Damozel (p. 451), awakens to the dangers of being a shallow American beauty and shocks her puritan mother by recommending that young women read Balzac, Maupassant, and Bourget before marriage, especially to a man of the world, if they expect to hold their husbands. Mabel is nearly a tragic figure because her wisdom arrives too late to overcome her early self-limitation.

In *Tower of Ivory*, Mrs. Atherton improves her control of the diverse elements of her long novels. Styr's singing the role of Isolde in Munich and her presentation of the whole range of Wagnerian heroines in London, designed by Ordham to awaken the respectable and sensuous English audience to Wagner's new music, unify the novel's dual setting and theme. The images of the potters, of ivory as an aesthetic aloofness from primal instincts, and of the effect of romantic Munich on respectable London help to give the novel a necessary cohesiveness that in previous novels was achieved by the author's dividing the narrative into parts. The last chapter, merely stating Ordham's diplomatic success and the curious public's assessment of his apparently young heart, is an anticlimactical tying up of loose ends of the plot. Gertrude Atherton named *Tower of Ivory* her favorite novel, probably because it most completely expressed her ideal union of the passion and spirit of a woman.[13]

IV Julia France and Her Times:
"The Joy of Succeeding"

Like *Patience Sparhawk*, *Julia France and Her Times* (1912) portrays the initiation of a young woman raised in an isolated civilization into experience in a developed one. Julia France

enlarges further than Betty Madison does a social and political
role for woman by learning to know herself and then by acting
politically in order to influence the election of the lawmakers.
Julia's development as a self-respecting individual, who recognizes that the "joy of succeeding" lies in study, work, and effort,
leads her into campaigning as a Suffragist in England as well as
into marriage to a man whom she loves.

Julia's times of innocence begin on Nevis, the birth isle of her
ancestor, Alexander Hamilton. There, because of an astrological
prediction of her high destiny, her ambitious mother forces on
her a marriage to Harold France, a dissipated heir-presumptive
to an English dukedom and currently a naval officer. Before the
marriage is consummated, Julia travels to London, where she is
trained for her role as a duchess by her aunt, Maria Winstone,
and where three young friends—"potters"—vow to "save"
innocent Julia from the intellectual and financial restrictions
associated with being a traditional English wife. Nigel Herbert, a
writer of novels on poverty, tries to persuade her to escape with
him to America. Bridget Herbert and Ishbel Jones, energetic,
strong-minded wives with no financial restrictions, awaken to
their need to become self-supporting and independent by their
own effort; they open a fashionable millinery shop. There they
give Julia experience—"little lessons" in life outside the "conventional early Victorian walls of her present destiny." Yet
dutiful Julia nurses back to health her now-retired husband, and
to his disdain further develops her intellect by reading.

Despite her passively expecting a high destiny through
marriage, Julia's knowledge increases. She learns the tenants'
side of English landowning policy, and becomes acquainted with
American social views through tourists who visit English estates,
among whom is Daniel Tay, a Californian. She is alternately
admired and neglected by her husband, who wins an election to
Parliament and then resorts to his earlier drunkenness and
neurotic torment of Julia when his cousin the duke marries,
produces an heir, and eliminates France from a dukedom. Julia's
belief in happiness in marriage and in her high destiny having
been proven false, she leaves her husband because of his insane
attack on the duke, and she seeks another source of knowledge
and happiness in a four-year study of Eastern religion in India.

On her return to London in 1906, Julia, influenced by Bridget
Herbert, now skeptically active with Fabian Socialists, joins the

Woman's War on poverty by campaigning for Liberal candidates with the Suffragists. Julia's new activity is motivated by her consciousness that, for her, mystical religion is a "fool's paradise," and by her recognition that women need political power in order to send men to Parliament who will fulfill their promises and eliminate the poverty of women and children laborers. As a Suffragist, she passively endures the scorn of hostile crowds, is jailed, and is surprisingly protected—on secret orders of the duke—when she participates with the Suffragists who storm Parliament in session.

At one of Julia's Suffragist lectures, Daniel Tay, now a successful San Francisco businessman, appears, and their youthful interest develops into love. This growth of love, her insistence on standing alone, France's commitment to an asylum, and the sudden death of the duke and his child further increase her consciousness of needing a "sense of humor" about life's paradoxes and her own power of self-deception. Convinced that Julia's husband cannot live long, Ishbel, now Lady Dark, persuades Julia and Daniel Tay to go to Nevis. On that still-innocent isle, Julia tests her acquired knowledge of human nature and her new belief in woman's independent role as she confronts the archetypal woman—the seductress—who is her niece, Fanny, who has enchanted Tay. With the aid of therapeutic hypnotism learned in India, Julia frees Fanny from her learned obsession with coquetry, and sends her to England for experience and knowledge. With the news of France's death, Julia decides to join her life actively with the plans of Tay to rebuild San Francisco.

The narrative of Julia France's life camouflages, for the reader of 1912, Mrs. Atherton's serious and ironic treatment of the historical effects of the socialization of women in Western civilization. The novelist observed that women born with energy, ambition, and intellectual ability but deprived of an outlet for these capabilities tend to scorn their sex. Idealized women, like Julia at first, have exaggerated expectations of their social and personal destiny; women's destiny is identified usually by false sources of knowledge, such as fixed social customs, religious dogma, or astrology, and women attain success primarily through conflict with other women for a man. However, through varied experiences that include work and the search for the "right" mate, Julia France, Ishbel Jones, and Bridget Herbert aid each other as some men aid other men, and discover, as do some men, the "sensation of self respect" (p. 110) and the liberty to choose their own fate. Julia's sense of humor about her conflicting desires, Ishbel's "bluffing herself" in good and bad situations, and Bridget's "enthusiasm" for usefulness to society exemplify their strategies for attaining their goals. They predict a future woman who will choose happiness alone or in a self-supporting and intense personal partnership in marriage (p. 420).

Julia France is Mrs. Atherton's typical woman, whose latent potentialities, somewhat exaggerated, lie less in her hereditary beauty and intellect and more in her losing her self-deception about her purpose in living. Once Julia awakens to the insignificance for her of a traditional woman's dependence on marriage alone for happiness and self-fulfillment, she begins to act out the psychological stages of a woman's developing ego. In Mrs. Atherton's opinion, that process includes acceptance of her own sex; a desire to know and to separate the illusive from the true; wanting to be self-supporting and useful in some great "impersonal cause" (p. 515); yearning for the right man but needing to stand alone to fulfill her inner self; and finally, with a sense of humor, to resolve her conflict between an impersonal cause and her desire to marry, to have children, and to aid a man in his work. In the depiction of Julia's maturation, fatuous as it seems at certain stages, Mrs. Atherton was criticizing current psychological novels, which in her opinion thrust the "modern thinking" man and woman into each other's arms at the end of a forced situation "with their natures unchanged ... [and] their inner problems unsolved" (p. 418). She also forecast the creation of heroines in later novels who would carry out what Julia analyzes in this novel.

This long novel is unified in its six books by the theme of woman's maturing enough to discover her own capabilities and to choose her goal. In Book I, the outmoded notions of Julia's mother handicap her daughter's growth. In Books II to V, the three potters in London (Bridget and Ishbel resemble two Suffragist friends of the author)[14] and the three men in Julia's life, representing respectively traditional marriage, religious passivity, and energetic progressivism, comprise the landmarks of Julia's education. The last book, narrating Fanny's unthinking coquetry, which Julia has the power and knowledge to transform, suggests that women can evolve if they share their experiences with their own kind. The allusive weaving of historical events in the 1890s and early 1900s—such as the Boer War, the San Francisco earthquake, and the militant Suffragist campaign—into the background and into certain incidents that affect the characters, adds cohesiveness to the novel

The motive of *Julia France and Her Times* began in a drama with a feminist role which Minnie Maddern Fiske asked Gertrude Atherton to write for her. Mrs. Atherton had to admit that she had no dramatic brain cells with which to bring to life the lives of the "Grim Crusaders" like the Pankhursts. The play received poor notices on its premiere performance in Montreal, and though the novel is dedicated "To Mrs. Fiske," the novelist remarked in her autobiography that although it gave a comprehensive view of the Woman's Movement in England, she "had no love for it" herself.[15]

V Perch of the Devil: *"The Spirit of Romance*
in the Money Makers of Today"

Perch of the Devil (1914) utilizes Montana as the "new most romantic subdivision of the United States" (p. 16) to replace the now classic California as the backdrop for depicting the "modern spirit of Western America." The era of exploitation of copper-mines like Perch of the Devil and the spectacular personalities of the state's mining era provide the background for a novel of the great middle class with a money-maker as the modern romantic hero and with a woman of the middle class, educated and refined and capable of doing her own housework, as a heroine who replaces the author's heretofore favored aristocratic type.

Gregory Compton, son of a New York farmer, taciturn, strong-willed, desiring the romance of mining on his ranch and ambitious to "do" something for Montana, marries beautiful Ida Hook, daughter of a miner and a laundress. Gregory's best friend and business partner, Mark Blake, marries a woman whom he has idealized, Ora Stratton. She embodies the attributes of Mrs. Atherton's "average American princess" of New England and Southern ancestry, educated but self-deluding in her search for a life purpose. The friendship of the men leads to a tutorial friendship between the women, and eventually to a rivalry between them for the love of Gregory. Ida and Ora educate each other in the areas each knows best, and they tour Europe for

more than a year in order to broaden Ida's experience and to
escape the marital ennui produced by the neglect of their
ambitious, busy husbands.

On their return from Europe, Ora decides to end her loveless
marriage, to continue her imagined ideal love of Gregory, who
harbors a similar ideal love of her, and to take an active interest
in her mine, adjacent to Gregory's Perch. Ida, newborn by her
European adventure, quickly assumes the middle-class social
leadership in Butte, a position that her role as wife of a
prosperous miner offers her. Despite her husband's neglect of
her, Ida refuses to divorce Gregory and challenges Ora to admit
that her idealization of Gregory has been a "fool's paradise."
After their dramatic confrontation deep in the mine, Ora returns
to Europe to marry an Italian nobleman who will satisfy the
demands of her type. Ida and Gregory find happiness as life
companions, interdependent but free to maintain their own
individualities and interests within marriage.

In this novel of the middle class, Mrs. Atherton creates two
new types of characters and places them in a new setting—the
bustling small town of Butte where the interaction of industry
and society could be observed in order to show a new stage in the
material progress of Western civilization. In the romance of
mining, Gregory is the adventuring engineer and the businessman with the boldest imagination; he is the "doing" buccaneer of
his time, the self-made man who discovers copper ore on his own
ranchland, purchases more land on which to build a railroad,
maintains his wife in luxury and neglect, and singlehandedly and
successfully confronts the huge Amalgamated Corporation,
which tries to pirate his veins of ore. In the romance of the heart,
Gregory is traditional man, torn between the passionate and
ideal woman, but he finally awakens to the role in marriage that
a new middle-class woman offers—an interesting life companion
and an entrepreneur of social relations.

Ida Hook represents a modern middle-class Helen, who
becomes an interesting individual by balancing her physical
attributes and her social and intellectual development. By
learning about her husband's mining and business responsibilities
and by interweaving them and the social activities of Butte as
much for her own pleasure as for aid to her husband, Ida
demonstrates that a woman contributes to the material progress
of civilization. For the first time, Mrs. Atherton allows her

heroine to express a desire for children, and at the same time discredits her favored type of aristocratic, idealizing heroine as an "atavistic" American, who fails to outgrow her need of admiring attention. Ida Compton is Mrs. Atherton's tribute to the versatile, self-reliant middle-class American woman, who, she thought, would equal the European lady.[16] One critic spoke of Ida as "a convincing person," deserving to stand in the "galaxy of American heroines" beside Robert Grant's Selma White, Theodore Dreiser's Carrie Meeber, and Edith Wharton's Lily Barth.[17]

Mrs. Atherton presents the engineering, metallurgical, and financial aspects of mining as convincingly as she does the social details of costuming and entertaining. A mining engineer and an expert on irrigation in Helena to whom the novel is dedicated verified her details. She evokes the austerity as well as the "cool polaric blue" beauty of Montana. In the same way that she utilizes the earthquake as a metaphor of regeneration in *Ancestors,* she portrays Montana's warm Chinook wind as capable of changing rigid human attitudes and of thawing wintry landscapes. *Perch of the Devil* marked a high point of achievement that the author herself later acknowledged she did not regain until the publication of her novel *Black Oxen* in 1923.

CHAPTER 5

Black Oxen: *"Living After the Jewels Had Given Out"*

G ERTRUDE Atherton's keen journalistic sensitivity to social and psychological undercurrents in the public's consciousness frequently rescued her from recurrent dry periods of her imagination. All of her novels to 1915 carried underneath the major plot movement traces of romance, mystery, and contemporary notions appealing particularly to the reader of popular fiction. *Patience Sparhawk* not only contains a realistic analysis of a new psychological phenomenon—the new woman in a romance—but also reflects public interest in mystery-crime stories, such as those of Arthur Conan Doyle. Echoing Robert Louis Stevenson and Anthony Hope's Ruritanian theme, *Rulers of Kings* (1904) portrays not a swashbuckling Englishman but a go-getter American businessman, a hero who triumphs over feudal-minded Europeans. Like the stories of Winston Churchill and James Lane Allen, Mrs. Atherton's California novels and her stories in *The Splendid Idle Forties* (1902) give the American past an aura of historical romance. Her heroines' struggles not to be dominated in love resemble the conflict of the sexes for power in the popular domestic novels of the nineteenth century.

To hold her audience during a period after 1915 when her creative tract was dormant and the world was disrupted by war, Mrs. Atherton relied on her considerable ability to appeal to popular taste in reading, and she expressed in newspaper articles, mystery stories, and novels her opinions on war, patriotism, socialism, women and war, and Freudian notions. Then *Black Oxen*, the best-seller that displaced Sinclair Lewis's *Babbitt* in 1923,[1] marked the return of her imaginative power.

Before *Black Oxen*, however, she published four books, three subtitled "A Novel," and one subtitled "A Mystery Story." In these she appeared to be experimenting with mystery as a narrative device and to treat her California material in the light of current social and economic forces. Reflecting a murder trial that Mrs. Atherton covered for a New York newspaper, *Mrs. Balfame, A Novel* (1916) deals with the effect on the accused character of press coverage of a crime in a suburb of New York, as well as with the solving of the mystery of the husband's murder. *The Avalanche, A Mystery Story* (1919) utilizes the author's perennial interest in a person's purpose in life as the serious fictional motive underneath the mystery that surrounds the parentage of her California heroine. A result of her long observations of German men and women and of German militarism, *The White Morning, A Novel of the Power of German Women in Wartime* (1918) imagines a revolt by women that will hasten the end of the war; whereas the essays of *The Living Present* (1917) describe the war work of French women in one part, and from that observation predict in the second an active feminism in Europe and America in the future. Attempting to recapture the author's previous achievement with her San Francisco setting and characters, *The Sisters-in-Law* (1921) and *Sleeping Fires* (1922) embroil both characters and the city in the effects of socialism, postwar adjustments, and the popularized notion of psychological inhibition.

Two novels, spinning off from the endocrinological theme of *Black Oxen*, are *The Crystal Cup* (1925) and *The Sophisticates* (1931). The first deals with a Freudian theme of sexual repression, which H. L. Mencken relegated to the Gland School of fiction.[2] The second, a novel of murder which Mrs. Atherton intended as a satire,[3] shows the reactions of the characters in a small midwestern town to a husband's murder and to the possibility of rejuvenation through a high-frequency treatment of the pituitary gland.[4] None of these works, except *Black Oxen*, added to Mrs. Atherton's literary reputation, but her "grasp of a new thing" and "her sense of timing" in appealing to the "mass impulse" of the general public kept her readers and the book reviewers aware of her.[5]

I   *"Years Like Great Black Oxen"*

Black Oxen (1923) epitomizes Gertrude Atherton's conception of the novel—a *mise-en-scène*, a powerfully realized principal

character, and a plan of life. For five years there had lurked in
Mrs. Atherton's imagination a beautiful, authoritative "European
but subtly American" woman, standing in a theater with her back
to the stage and surveying the audience on the opening night of a
new play.[6] No appropriate theme or plan of life stimulated Mrs.
Atherton to realize this "graceful, arresting mysterious figure"
until the publicity surrounding the rejuvenation treatment of Dr.
Steinach of Vienna catapulted the mysterious figure out of her
imagination into the fictional world of New York in the 1920s.[7]
Fifty-eight-year-old Countess Marie Zattiany of Hungary, née
Mary Ogden of New York, appearing to be thirty after a Steinach
treatment, brings this figure to life to face the universal problem
of handling the "years like Great Black Oxen" that prod the
human being toward his destiny. In *Black Oxen*, Mrs. Atherton
wrote a significant novel in which the game of romance loses to
real life. The heroine epitomizes the importance of the creation
of a lifelong purpose in order to have a reason for "living after
the jewels had given out."[8]

Every incident and almost every conversation and interior
monologue contribute to the central dilemma that faces Mary
Zattiany, as she comes to be known in the novel—the choice
which she must make between a return to youth and love
through marriage to thirty-four-old Lee Clavering and a capture
of political power through marriage to Prince Hohenauer of
Austria. Her choice is determined ultimately by her undeluded
realization that "power, after sex has ceased from troubling, is
the dominant passion in human nature" (p. 336). The novel
consists of fifty-nine chapters, but its movement in time is
concentrated into two seasons: the winter in which Madame
Zattiany's past experience is revealed, her impact on New York
society is described, and her engagement to Clavering is
announced; and the spring when Mary's experienced mind casts
off the dubious prospect of happiness in romantic love in favor of
political and social significance in Vienna. Associating romantic
love with winter and death in this novel ironically reverses the
popular expectation of love in springtime when Mary renounces
love for power.

The tension in the novel, as much mental as emotioinal, arises
from Mary's willfully self-deluding attempt to play the American
game of romantic love with Clavering, even though she has
devoted most of her life to the European games of gallantry,

"where men make a definite cult of women and women of men" (p. 55), and has reaped only disillusionment. She has returned incognito to her birthplace, New York, after forty years in Europe in order to regain control of her American fortune. Although she does not expect to reacquaint herself with the friends of her youth, her gesture in the theater arouses the curiosity of the Sophisticates, a bohemiam group of young writers and artists led by Lee Clavering, a journalist and playwright. Her resemblance to the well known Mary Ogden of the 1880s involves her in a round of social activities that leads inevitably to her revealing her identity to her old friends, who have dutifully carried out the traditional woman's duties to their children and grandchildren; the last include the current flappers and sports of the jazz age. Then perversely discarding her European experience, Mary indulges herself in giving the game of love another chance, this time with the American Lee Clavering. Only Gora Dwight, the novelist and friend of Clavering, objectively observes that Mary's love is a reckless phase.

Lee and Mary's bacchanalian celebration of their engagement with a group of the Sophisticates in a lodge in the Adirondacks is interrupted by the arrival of Prince Hohenauer; he insists upon seeing Mary and precipitates her choice between love and power. The prince, her lover in the past, pierces Mary's self-deluding game: "You have been able to deceive yourself here in the country of ... [your] girlhood, for a time, with this interesting young gentleman in love with you" (p. 324). Because he is now planning to make Vienna the postwar capital of a great and influential republic, the prince offers her the opportunity to "become the most powerful woman in Europe" as his wife. He reminds her that marriage to Clavering would erase the identity and opportunity that had made her significant politically and socially in Europe through her past marriage to Count Zattiany. Later, in the last meeting with Clavering, who loves her as deeply as his idea of male dominance allows, Mary's old mind pulls away from his young one. Like a Shavian drama, the novel ends abruptly as the lovers almost casually part.

II *Flappers and Sophisticates*

New York as a post war *mis-en-scène* of the 1920s had two

highly visible preoccupations: One of the cult of youth, in which
the "lost generation" was glorified and the flapper was
glamorized; and the other was the fashionableness of sex,
resulting from the popularization of Freud and the widely
publicized revolution in sexual morals and manners. In the novel,
three generations of restless New Yorkers react to the sensational appearance of young-old Mary Zattiany. Men of all ages
admire her vitality and beauty. Women of different ages react
according to their assumptions about what youth and age, love
and sex, mean in women's lives. Mary's rejuvenation also affects
the attitudes of several social groups—the older society of
fashion in which Mary spent her youth in the 1880s and about
which Edith Wharton wrote in *The Age of Innocence*; the newer
smart set of self-amusing, self-aggrandizing artists and writers,
the Sophisticates; the flappers in their newly emancipated youth
and sex. By drawing the American-European aristocratic Mary
Zattiany into the Sophisticates, who go to the theater, discuss
books, art, and drama, and dance and dine in public places as well
as in private homes, Mrs. Atherton contrasts the American and
European notions of sophistication, the new and the old society
of New York and the role of the traditional woman with that of
an unconventional woman and the flapper. Mary's knowledge of
European politics and war contrasts with the limited interest of
fashionable society and the Sophisticates in the problems facing
the world. This indifference and self-centeredness are symbolized by the Sophisticates' retreat to the illusion of male-
dominated primitivism in the Adirondacks—an illusion destroyed
by the intrusion of the Austrian prince, representative of the
complexities of civilization.

   In this milieu, Mary Zattiany is Mrs. Atherton's "powerfully
realized character," who after a loveless marriage and bitter
disappointments in Europe comes to realize "the tragic futility"
of a life spent in search of love. An ambitious woman in a man's
world, she has discovered long since that her sexual magnetism is
her most powerful political weapon. However, she cannot satisfy
her desire for power by direct political action because, as Prince
Hohenauer reminds her, "masculine jealousy" keeps women
from doing more than "pulling hidden strings" (p. 322). Even
though sex is an obsolescent political tool that loses effectiveness
with the approach of age and decline of beauty, Mary has
learned to manipulate men as a musical instrument from which

she can evoke "any harmony or cacophony she chose" (p. 166). In the harsh world of politics, she knows that she must use sexual power in order to gain the opportunity to employ her intelligence, her political finesse, and her knowledge of the affairs of state.

A withered old woman devastated by the war and a relic of the nineteenth-century idea of woman before returning to New York, Mary, restored to youth in the frenzied world of the 1920s, raises the question of what she—or any woman or man—can or will do with a new chance to find happiness. Although Mary appears to embody all that a woman can dream of attaining and possessing—beauty, magnetism, wisdom, experience, love, power—she still deludes herself about love. Except for playing this game of youthful love with Clavering, with herself as chief audience of her performance (p. 321), Mary is a fixed character. This static figure, watching her own delusion, emphasizes the novel's challenge to women's assumptions about youth and sex, and throws the dynamics of action to the characters who react to her.

Two other major "flat" characters function as foils to Mary and as additional points of view on the reaction of New York to her. Lee Clavering and Gora Dwight as literary artists represent respectively a romantic and a realistic view of the relationship between man and woman in regard to love, sex, and youth. Clavering, a romantic Southerner holding the traditional notions about manners and about man as artist and master of woman, possesses an "old mind" in a young body. While he attracts the affection of three generations of women, the love impulse between him and Mary, because of his possessiveness and ego and because of her past experience in love, leads to a protracted battle of wills. He deludes himself that Mary will sacrifice her ambitions for a political career in Europe and live happily with him in New York, where his career ambitions lie. Gora Dwight alerts him to his dangerous mistake. Her unhappy experience in love, recounted in *The Sisters-in-Law*, has been compensated for by her success as a popular Realistic novelist. She prefers independence in her social and professional life and in a companionable relationship with men; hence she, as objective novelist, observes human nature as it is, and warns the lovers of their delusion about finding complete happiness.

III   *Sex: Freedom, Rivalry, and Social Duty*

In depicting women from eighteen to sixty years of age, all of whom react to Mary Zattiany's new opportunities at fifty-eight, Gertrude Atherton dramatizes not only the nature of the effect of the decade's obsessions with youth, age, and sex, but also the effect on women of their unexamined conceptions of themselves and their social duty. When Mary's identity is revealed, the friends of her own age, their offspring, and their friends begin to show deep concern about the effect of their beliefs on their lives. The characterizations of three generations of one family—Jane Oglethorpe; her son, Jim; his ineffectual wife, Molly; and Janet, her granddaughter—emphasize the frequently destructive effect of inherited ideas on personal identity and human relationships.

Janet Oglethorpe, the eighteen-year-old flapper, self-assured that the world of "having fun" and even an "old tyre" like Lee Clavering belong to her, at first does not perceive Mary Zattiany as her sexual rival for Lee. On the announcement of the engagement, Janet's self-asserted emancipation and her anger at an older woman's "sneaking young girls' lovers away" result in her attempting an old female ploy to compromise a man into marrying her: she stages a scene in Clavering's apartment. Although Clavering rationalizes that Janet's "new freedom" merely reflects the disillusion of the young people with the hollow results of the recent world war, he advises Jim Oglethorpe, her father, not to continue to be a "backseat parent" and to take his daughter to Europe for education in the larger world.

Janet's words and behavior in the novel display not only the limited use to which a flapper might put her new freedom, but also her absolute equation of youth and sex and her narrow conception of her potential as a woman. Her grandmother as a mother of eight children and a society leader, her own mother as a submissive wife and "backseat parent," and her carousing peers provide feminine models for Janet that are defined only in relationship to men. As a sixty-year-old novelist, Gertrude Atherton would recall in Janet Oglethorpe her own undisciplined childhood and parental neglect and the exaggerated value that American culture has placed upon youth in women.[9]

Several New York women in their twenties, more sophisticated and sensitive than Janet and attracted also to Lee Clavering, perceive Mary as a sexual rival and regard youth in women as the time for bearing children, an achievement that they cattily remark is impossible for Mary. To Anne Goodrich's query at Mary's dinner for the young women, "And what else does youth in women really mean?" Clavering responds, perhaps for Mrs. Atherton, "Experience has taught me that it means quite a number of other things" (p. 223).

The friends of Mary's youth observe her rejuvenation not as a direct sexual rivalry but as a renewed opportunity for love and sex at maturity. At the same time they acknowledge that the vibrant Mary as their contemporary in age painfully proves their own outmoded position in the society. They are both disgusted and fascinated by Mary's description of her rejuvenation as an "interior drama," which they perceive as an "abnormal renaissance" of "that section which refined women ceased to discuss after they had got rid of it" (p. 139).

Sixty-year-old Jane Oglethorpe and forty-two-year-old Agnes Trevor, living according to nineteenth-century codes of self-sacrificing marital duty and genteel purity in women, confess to Lee Clavering and Mary Zattiany the repression that these codes have cost them. Clavering early in the novel muses about the extent of the popularization of Freudian ideas in America: "He knew barely another woman [only Gora Dwight] who did not get around to sex sooner or later. Psychoanalysis has relieved them of whatever decent inhibitions they might have had in the past" (p. 62). And Mary's rejuvenation breaks down the barriers of the most reserved of older women, including Agnes Trevor. Agnes had left society in her early twenties, devoting herself to "moralizing the East side," and gradually losing her prudishness about sex as she watched the settlement girls grow and marry. Her repression and "superb self-control" shattered by Mary's sympathy, Agnes is "swept back into the dark vortex of her secret past." She moans, "Oh, I tell you that unless I can be young again and have some man—any man—I don't care whether he'll marry me or not—I'll go mad—mad" (pp. 263-64). Mary's advice to the smartly dressed patrician woman, sprawled on her sofa, to regain her vanity and self-respect by ignoring what other people expect of her, forces Mary to reconsider her own position. This scene brings on the novel's denouement in the springtime retreat to the Adirondacks and the appearance of Prince Hohenauer.

Mary's opportunity, after her unconventional life in Europe, to live again as a young woman brings to the surface Jane Oglethorpe's resentment against her life of marital and social duty, her concern about her granddaughter's behavior, and the ignominy of old age. To Clavering, the widowed Jane confesses that she is "a terribly bewildered old woman," capable of loving again but unable to attract any emotion but "impeccable respect" from a man.

My heart is as young today as Mary Ogden's .... I'd give my immortal soul to be thirty again—or look it. I meant thirty and all I know now. ... I'm not so damn sure I'd have tried to make myself think I was in love with James [her husband] .... I'd have found out what love and life meant, that's what! And when I did I'd have sent codes and traditions to the devil. (pp. 195-96).

Clavering, an objective artist, might be speaking for Mrs. Atherton when he remarks that the diminished life of a dutiful woman like Jane Oglethorpe holds greater tragedy than Mary Zattiany's misfortune in marriage and war (p. 196).

These women's responses to Mary's rejuvenation comprise Mrs. Atherton's evidence of the destructiveness to women of their continuing dependence on a man for self-identity and on an equation of love and sex with youth. Only Mary and Gora Dwight offer alternative and lifelong purposes for women. Gora's unhappy love affair, her exclusion from San Francisco society because of her liberal ideas, and her experience with war and death, all related in *The Sisters-in-Law*, free her to develop her own abilities. After the success of her realistic novel of life in a small interior town in California, titled *Fools*, Gora moves to New York to continue her career in a freer environment. In *Black Oxen*, Gora and Mary embody a new myth of woman, one who lives through or transcends the demands of sexuality, and channels individual effort into artistic and intellectual achievement. In the sense that human happiness results from an individual's full development and lifelong purpose, the novel adds an optimistic tone to the image from William Yeats's poem of "years like Great Black Oxen" treading the world.

IV   *"The Curse of Imagination"*

Gertrude Atherton's rendering of an innocent New York at a later time than that of Edith Wharton's *The Age of Innocence* and its dealing with society more fully than F. Scott Fitzgerald's *The Great Gatsby* result in a "brilliantly" executed panorama, according to one critic.[10] Her theme of innocence is a psychological as well as a social one, and the creation of different types of characters allows the reader to react to their psychological states. Lee Clavering is both romantic and predatory as a lover; Mary Zattiany is both arrogant and sympathetic in her image of an independent, experienced woman still desiring love; Jane Oglethorpe is both tragic and pathetic as the obsolescent older woman rejected by society. The plan of life so essential to Mrs. Atherton's novels accurately reflects the human need to love and to be loved and to feel worthwhile throughout life. Through the characters' reactions to Mary's rejuvenation and through her rejection of romantic love in favor of derived political power, Mrs. Atherton in this novel makes her strongest criticism of the Western ideal of supreme and total fulfillment in love because it enslaves women mentally and physically. The narrator describes this "fool's paradise":

No woman had ever lived who was more completely disillusioned, more scornful of that age-old dream of human happiness, which, stripped to its bones, was merely the blind instinct of the race to survive. Civilization had heaped its fictions over the bare fact of nature's original purpose, imagination lashing generic sexual impulse to impossible demands for the consummate union of mind and soul and body. . . . Life itself was futile enough, but that dream of the perfect love between two beings immemorially paired was the most futile and ravaging of all the dreams civilization had imposed upon mankind. The curse of imagination. Only the savages and the ignorant masses understood 'love' for the transitory functional thing it was and were undisturbed by spiritual unrest . . . by dreams . . . mad longing. . . . (pp. 56-57)

Thus *Black Oxen* exploded the motive force of romance behind the happy endings of popular fiction. At the same time that its theme of rejuvenation and sexuality led to its being banned in several cities, it achieved the status of a best-seller, a status that Gertrude Atherton did not achieve again in twenty more years of writing. In a movie version of the novel in 1924, Corrine Griffith became a star.[11]

Although in *Black Oxen* Mrs. Atherton primarily portrayed the delusions about youth and sex held by upper-class women in New York, she received hundreds of letters from women scattered all over the United States, England, and the colonies. Mostly the correspondents were journalists, teachers, and women trying to hold jobs—all asking her aid in achieving a renewal of energy such as Mary Zattiany's in order to continue to work and to live without fatigue. This wide response may indicate that the novelist successfully adapted her style to a sensational idea so that she could reach the deeper concern of her readers. The challenge of her question of youth-age and the readers' apprehension of its significance both show how effectively Mrs. Atherton unified the idea and controlled her sometimes uneven and turgid style. One critic praised her capacity to absorb the spirit of her time and to present characters as "living people talking and acting like living people in that day."[12]

CHAPTER 6

Resurrected History: "The Past as an Exercise for the Imagination"

W RITING as a conventional historian to celebrate the Pan-Pacific Exposition in San Francisco in 1915, Gertrude Atherton published *California: An Intimate History* at the end of 1914. In it, she recorded her choice of the main historic events of the state and their causes and illuminated them through her intimate knowledge of California history and personalities.[1] However, like most historians, in that history she had to omit "glimpses of the inner men," the details of the private and social lives of the people involved.

Then in 1926, after more than three decades of believing that novelists were the best current historians, she turned again to the form of the biographical historical novel that she had invented in 1902, and in which she had resurrected the life of "unordinary" characters of the past, such as Alexander Hamilton, for the benefit of posterity.[2]

In three historical novels written in the late 1920s, and dealing with personalities of classical times, Mrs. Atherton added to the historical detail of scene and event her imagination of the inner selves of well-known historical characters. As she had done in *The Conqueror*, she connected the psychological study of her characters to her aim to be a "correct historian" of her own times by permitting her narrator the opportunity to view the personalities and events of the ancient period from a current and unsentimental perspective. She demonstrated her versatility as a historian-fictionist in presenting the famous love story and morganatic marriage of Aspasia and Pericles in *The Immortal Marriage* (1927); in portraying the ambitious Alcibiades in *The Jealous Gods, A Processional Novel of the 5th Century B.C. (Concerning One Alcibiades)* (1928); and in singing of arms and

109

the woman in *Dido, Queen of Hearts* (1929), her contribution to the Virgil Bimillennium. To these she added a fiction with historical setting, *Golden Peacock* (1936), dealing with a plot against Augustus.

In a literary decade featuring America's lost generation and the debunking of classical times, as in John Erskine's *The Private Life of Helen of Troy*, Mrs. Atherton's novels resurrected the ancient ideals as they were explained by both ancient and modern writers on those times. Because of her narrative focus on the inner lives of her characters, she revealed further evidence of her belief in unchanging human nature and in the multifaceted genius of historical persons. Her most appreciative audience for these novels came from college students and professors and teachers of the classics.

I   The Immortal Marriage:
"Much Joy in Being a Biographical Novelist"

The theme of *The Immortal Mariage* (1927) is the love and intellectual relationship of the famous leader, Pericles of Athens, and the beautiful, intellectual "foreigner," Aspasia of Miletus. Aspasia as much as Pericles inspired the novel. Based on more than two hundred books that Mrs. Atherton read on Pericles and his times and in which Aspasia is merely alluded to, the novel recreates Pericles' supreme accomplishments as the political leader of Athens and as arbiter of the conflict between the Oligarchs and Demos, as the successful warrior, as orator in the name of democracy, and as political target of the comic poets (who used his relationship with Aspasia to attack his regime). Observed through Aspasia's eyes, Pericles is lover, husband, intellectual companion, father, and guardian of Greek youth, including Alcibiades.

Arriving in Athens, Aspasia teaches Socrates and other prominent Athenians. She lives outwardly according to the customs of upper-class Athenian women and inwardly according to her own independent attitudes. Her bond of friendship with Pericles, her loving him, their "morganatic marriage,"[3] the birth of their son, her loneliness while he fights at sea or against Sparta, and her active participation in his political oratory and action—all of these are interwoven with the known historical events and personalities of the Golden Age of Athens. Aspasia's account of a greater Dionysia, when Sophocles' trilogy and satire won the prize, her listening to Sophocles reading his tragedies, her trial for her outspoken disbelief in the gods, and Pericles' eloquent and tearful defense of her recreate Aspasia's place in this momentous era of Athens. The novel ends with Pericles' funeral at which a now dependent Aspasia attempts to recall in Pindar's words the vital man, "the creator of a day, the dream of a shadow."

The obvious love story gives to the novel a structure of four books: a love alliance of two independent persons, both intellectual and passionate; the birth of their son and Aspasia's influence on Pericles' political and military leadership of Athens; Pericles' defense of himself and of Aspasia against the attack of the comic playwrights and others; and Aspasia's despair because of her declining independence and the death of Pericles. The lack of narrative suspense because of the known historical plot is overcome by the new characterization of Aspasia and by the narrator, who as a correct historian accurately sets the scene and wittily imagines comparisons between modern circumstances and those of the ancient times.

Aspasia's special endowment of intellect and beauty is explained by a dream in which Athene, a figure in ivory and gold, proclaims Aspasia her daughter and advises her to become an immortal ideal of woman, a virgin like the goddess, not needing a man for happiness. Aspasia, however, chooses mortality and Pericles, with whom she achieves an intimate companionship and reciprocal love—a relationship that contrasts with the Greek preference of a man-to-man ideal. In recording Aspasia's inner thoughts, the narrator subtly compares Greek and contemporary attitudes. Aspasia faces problems with her reasoning ability because she knows nothing, the narrator avers, about sentimentality or morbid introspection or suffering, contingencies of a woman's condition of a later age. In addition, Aspasia, with her passion for perfection, desires the complete and harmonious development of every part of her being:

She recalled the time when she had thought her life complete and took a serene pride in her unique gifts and position in Hellas. But she had lived with Pericles since! Her intellect and her great accomplishments were but a part of the whole, no longer dominant. And to give birth to a child, loved because it was the child of Pericles, would crumble the last blind wall in her being. (p. 223)

Thus Mrs. Atherton transformed the "historic fact" of Aspasia as *hetaera* to a new, unsentimental but romantic ideal—a fully developed woman, an ideal that ironically commented on woman's potential achievement in the hedonistic 1920s.

Desiring this book to be "accurate history as much as an interesting presentment of those greatest lovers of all times," Gertrude Atherton faithfully reproduced the scene, the atmosphere, and especially the cultural monuments of Athens. Aspasia attends the Theater of the Dionysia, praises the frieze and the gold and ivory statue of Athene in the temple of Athene Polias, and dares to walk through the "marble loveliness" of the agora with Pericles. The novelist imagines all of the scenes, letting historical facts stimulate her to recreate an era and living vicariouslly in it during the writing process. Although *The Immortal Marriage* promptly sold thirty thousand copies and continued to sell well for several years, in an age when the cinema was beginning to take the place of reading with a certain public the novel's myriad of detail, its leisurely pace, and its academic tone did not reach a wide audience as had *Black Oxen*.[4]

II   The Jealous Gods:
"A Fine Piece of Imaginative Reconstruction and Insight"

The Jealous Gods (1928), subtitled *A Processional Novel of the 5th Century B.C. (Concerning One Alcibiades)*, followed *The Immortal Marriage* immediately. Ostensibly its central theme is the procession of events after Pericles' death documenting the rise to success of Alcibiades in Athens and his assassination. Essentially it is a story of conflicts of power—between political entities, between city states and alien nations, but most of all between a man and a woman. A minor character in *The Immortal Marriage*, overshadowed by Pericles but admiring of Aspasia, Alcibiades arrogantly sets out to fulfill the high destiny that he believes has been promised by the gods' endowment of him with every virtue. With so much historical information already available on the aggressive, imperishable Alcibiades, Gertrude Atherton imagines a new antagonist for him to attempt to dominate. Tiy is a beautiful, intellectual, independent, and wealthy Egyptian woman, a descendant of famous women leaders. Tiy has come to Athens to win or to destroy Alcibiades. The interaction of the two strong and ambitious personalities permits the biographical novelist to reveal the inner thoughts and feelings of a historical and an imagined character and to compare a man and a woman in the procession to success.

The Jealous Gods follows Thucydides' version of Greek history in relating Alcibiades' lifelong scheming to become and to remain a leader of Athens and the effect of his success in making the gods jealous. His amorous adventures, his disdain of Athenian rituals, his shifting of alliances with Sparta and Persia, his exile from and return to Athens, and his assassination form the chronology of the novel. Between the episodes of his political and military actions, Alcibiades attempts to dominate Tiy. Tiy, on the other hand, attempts to show Alcibiades that with a little less arrogance he might be the greatest of men, and refuses to fill his empty hours until he is permanently exiled from Athens and they can together weave political plots. In Mrs. Atherton's rendition of the way that two ambitious characters exist, the novel explores the eternal question of an individual's life purpose. Tiy, like most of Mrs. Atherton's women characters who are independent of a relationship with a man, uses time profitably for her own purposes.

This second novel of fifth-century Athens offers slow-moving history, faithful description of scene and archaeology, and excellent comedy. The division of the novel into seven books indicates the structure of the procession to power and suggests a comic point of view. The comedy originates in the notion of confronting Alcibiades with an equally domineering Egyptian woman. Tiy is accustomed to treating the effeminate man, whom Egyptian women kept for their lighter hours, with the same sovereign contempt that the Athenians reserve for their women. In every book but the last, Tiy resists the amorous Alcibiades, consenting only to be his adviser and insisting there is little difference between the sexes. Such a confrontation affords not only comedy but opportunities to satirize social custom that are not lost on the reader. The historical details of life in Greece and Ionia, in Byzantium and Sicily, invite the reader to understand to some extent what these civilizations, established on a basis of slavery and the seclusion of women, were like.

In her autobiography, Mrs. Atherton expressed her joy in being a biographical novelist, completely happy when writing *The Immortal Marriage* and *The Jealous Gods* even while knowing that the public of the Machine Age, little interested in anything so remote as ancient Greece, would fail to make them popular. Critics, however, appreciated her accurate recreation of the period, one pointing to *The Jealous Gods* as "a fine piece of imaginative reconstruction and insight."[5]

III   Dido, Queen of Hearts:
"A Human as Well as a Tragic Figure"

Dido, Queen of Hearts (1929), written to celebrate the Virgil Bimillennium, combines the early story of Elissa of Tyre—who as Dido the wanderer founded the city of Carthage—with the legend invented by Virgil in Book Four of the *Aeneid*. A princess, Elissa is denied her chance to rule Tyre, and when her husband, Sychaeus, is murdered by her greedy brother, King Pygmalion, Elissa collects her husband's secret treasure (coveted by Pygmalion), some faithful nobles, and twenty biremes and escapes by sea. After Carthage is built, Dido's story begins to reflect the first four books of the Roman epic, but it takes on a romantic rather than the political and sentimental tone of Virgil's poem. With the blessing of Venus Astarte, Dido and Aeneas meet in the cave, and a brief, happy marriage ensues. When Mercury warns Aeneas that he must fulfill his god-decreed destiny, Aeneas dutifully prepares to sail. Dido plans her death on a pyre with Aeneas' forgotten shield and weapon, but not, as in the epic, because she could not face life without Aeneas. Simultaneously with Aeneas' departure, Iarbas, king of neighboring Libya, plans to marry Dido or to sack Carthage if she refuses his suit. Proclaiming her faithful noble Tadmalek, son of Hannibal, as king of Carthage, and falling on Aeneas' sword, Dido acts more as a queen giving her life for her people than as a woman preferring death to life without the love of a man.

The popular phrasing of the subtitle, "Queen of Hearts," suggests the structure of the novel and the characterization of Dido. Each of the four parts emphasizes the independent will and leadership of Dido as queen. Each part also unfolds the capacity to love—Sychaeus and Aeneas—and to transcend Virgil's epithet—"infelix Dido"—by showing that she holds the love of her people and of Tadmelak, her minister, who successfully negotiates with hostile Tyre. In contrast, Aeneas' minister, Achates, cannot persuade the King of Latium to help him to secure a kingdom for Iulus, Aeneas' son, so that Aeneas will not have to leave Dido and Carthage.

Impetuous and cautious, changeable and constant, Dido displays the various attributes of Mrs. Atherton's self-reliant heroines. And, like reprehensible Alcibiades, Dido escapes somewhat the paralyzing respect that the novelist shows toward the upstanding historical figures like Aspasia and Pericles. Dido's characterization as queen and lover makes her "a human and a tragic figure," while Aeneas in the words of one critic seems "something of a prig."[6] Despite the vivid evocation of scene and costume of that time and place and Mrs. Atherton's homage to Virgil, the story of Dido and Aeneas does not equal her literary imagination of Aspasia and Pericles and of Alcibiades and Tiy.

IV Golden Peacock:
"The Most Vivid and Believable of the Mediterranean Novels"

Golden Peacock (1936) is Mrs. Atherton's second novel (the first was *The Doomswoman*) to employ a first-person narrator. Pomponia, an invented sixteen-year-old niece of Horace, who calls her "golden peacock," relates a short portion of her life in 20 or 19 B.C., when the murder of her parents before her eyes begins the unfolding of a plot against Emperor Augustus of Rome.

Pomponia reveals her knowledge of Roman constitutional matters as learned from the age of four from Horace, Virgil, Polos, and Maecenas. She wittily comments on religious, social, and literary attitudes in Rome; endangers her life by spying on Julia, Augustus's daughter, the suspected perpetrator of the plot against the emperor; breaks up the intrigue; and at the end marries her lover, a Roman soldier. The fast-moving, exciting plot enlivens Pomponia's necessary monologues, which explain the background, action, and personalities involved. Mrs. Atherton's vigorous, colloquial style encourages the reader to accept the precocious narrator, who acts also as the author's unsentimental voice of "correct history" by commenting on Augustan attitudes that seem to prick equally at ancient and modern notions. In all of the historical novels, the narrator's skillful connection of past and present human behavior subtly indicates a certain fundamental unity of the human spirit.

V   *"The Imagination Fully Liberated"*

When writing a historical biographical novel, Gertrude Atherton declared that she "lived, breathed, slept in the past":

Every character of that period was a friend, acquaintance, or enemy, and I moved among them and listened to their voices.... In no other mental work—save no doubt poetry—is the imagination fully liberated.... Facts, far from hampering, are stimulants; each opens up a new vista.[7]

This genre, in part, resolved the novelist's concern for the lack of imagination in American literature. She thoroughly reimagined the historical background so that, according to Taine's precept, the characters in their public and private thoughts and acts stand out in bold relief. She exposed the intimate emotional acts of major and minor historical characters as evidence that human nature is unchanging. With each novel, she attempted to adjust the language of the times without sounding stilted or archaic. In each, her opening sentence stirs the imagination to expect an exciting narrative even though laid in the distant past. "The last thing that Alcibiades had wanted was to marry," opens *The Jealous Gods*, and only at the end of the novel is the reader rewarded with the union of Alcibiades and Tiy, lovers who deserve each other. Unfortunately, Mrs. Atherton wrote these historical novels in years when serious imaginative treatment of the past appealed only to a small public. Nonetheless, reviewers consistently agreed that she married fact and fiction without allowing one or the other to dominate.

CHAPTER 7

"Time's Cycle":
From California to California

ADVENTURES of a Novelist (1932) recapitulated Gertrude Atherton's life and times up to her permanent return to San Francisco in 1932. In this book of "reminiscences,"[1] Mrs. Atherton focuses primarily upon her own conception of her life as an adventuring writer in various places and times. Because her reminiscences are a kind of fiction, the shape that she chose to give her life and personality reveals much about the imagination that created the characters—women and men—in her fiction. In 1940 she returned again to her California material, utilizing its past and modern phases in two novels and two "histories" as if she were seeking to record the ultimate meaning of her cyclical quest. The two novels climax a series of eleven novels that features both a California woman and San Francisco as paradigms of decentralization in Western civilization—a movement from aristocracy to democracy.

In *The House of Lee* (1940), Mrs. Atherton telescopes a sixty-year history into several months in recounting the lives of three generations of California women in San Francisco from the 1860s to 1938; and in *The Horn of Life* (1942) she reexamines the quest of her favorite type of woman character for a lifelong purpose in San Francisco in the turbulent 1920s. Two retellings of past and present incidents and personalities of the Golden Gate area and of San Francisco—*Golden Gate Country* (1945) and *My San Francisco, a Wayward Biography* (1946)—end her writing career. These books provide additional evidence that she combined her creed of the imaginative and original writer with her questioning of life's purpose, and her eleven novels on California and more than twenty others, when observed as a

117

whole output, show how they were designed to extend her readers' knowledge of the great world.

I   Adventures of a Novelist: *"A Self-Portrait Free of Self-Justifying Sentimentality"*

In creating the heroines of her novels, Gertrude Atherton often combined autobiography with the projection of an idealized self-image as if she were attempting to work out the contrarieties and ambiguities that she recognized in herself and in her surroundings. In recalling events and people in her autobiography, she actually writes a memoir, for she records her memories of other people and places more than she describes her own thoughts and emotions. The details of the first thirty years of her life in California, described in the first quarter of the book, bring her personality into sharpest focus; thereafter she reveals herself primarily in her reactions to people and places.

The image that she presents of herself stresses two somewhat contradictory facets of her personality—facets that can also be detected in her heroines. She saw herself both as traditional woman, attending to aristocratic social amenities and appropriate relations with men, and as professional woman, supporting herself and remaining independent of marriage and domesticity. Priding herself on observing human nature as it is and on remaining aloof from whatever readers or reviewers thought of her, Mrs. Atherton treats her strengths and weaknesses with candor and wit, and is able to remark on the life and times of others with the same objectivity and bite with which she comments on her own foibles. One critic described the autobiography as "a self-portrait free of self-justifying sentimentality."[2]

In view of the fact that all of her papers and memorabilia were lost in the earthquake and fire in San Francisco in 1906, it is a remarkable feat of memory that Mrs. Atherton was able to recall so fully the details of the first fifty years of her life, the half century that occupies the first four and a half books of her nine-book autobiography. Uninterested in dates of events, possibly because of her vain disdain of aging, Mrs. Atherton nonetheless provides a generally accurate chronology, which allows a spontaneous association of events and personalities at different but contiguous times. This mode of selecting and ordering events in her adventures replicates her belief in "Time's cycles," in which human nature and history are unchanging, and explains why in her many novels the same themes and types of personalities recur.

The memoirs unfold by anecdote and by journalistic observation of scene and event. Superficial details of conversations with well-known personages abound, perhaps because of the author's insistent attention to social protocol.[3] But there are no deeper probing beyond the facade of manners and no critical evaluation of what she saw and heard.[4] She treats her conception of herself as she does her fictional characters, with authorial aloofness, and makes only cryptic comments on what she thought of her own work. The memoirs end abruptly with 1931, but the autobiography makes clear that Mrs. Atherton's conception of life is a lifelong quest for happiness.

II   The House of Lee: *"A General Leveling Up as Well as Down"*

In *The House of Lee* (1940), Gertrude Atherton tells of "the new poor," three generations of Lee women in San Francisco, who in 1938 because of their diminished inherited income must seek jobs to support themselves. In contrast with the poverty of the land-poor squatters in *Los Cerritos,* "the new poor" in this novel result from "the great leveler Depression," from the redistribution of wealth through the interaction of government, labor, and capital, and from the merging of social levels that occurred later in San Francisco than in New York. As in *Black Oxen,* Mrs. Atherton presents her chronicle of women's reactions against a new circumstance from three points of view within one family in order to demonstrate "time's cycle." The three are Mrs. Lucy Lee Edington, a sixty-year-old widow, whose father, a Virginia Lee, had come to California in 1852; Mrs. Lucy Lee, her forty-year-old widowed daughter; and her granddaughter, twenty-year-old Lucy Lee, who most resembles her grandmother.

This ancestral line inhabits the Lee mansion, built in the 1870s, "the most debased period of American architecture" (p. 18). The mansion has housed the first California Lee's fine library and private collection of paintings and marbles, some of which have had to be sold, and the house has served as a Southern aristocratic setting for great balls and dinners, presided over by Mrs. Edington until her husband's death. Now the house, like the three Lucys, must find a function appropriate to diminished circumstances. Each woman, facing herself in a mirror in her boudoir in the mansion, confronts anew the purpose of her life, a purpose once aristocratically defined, now necessarily democratic.

Even San Francisco, which in previous novels such as *The Californians* and *Ancestors* had prided itself on its aristocratic society, ensconced in mansions on Nob Hill, must adapt to changing conditions. The graceful architecture in both the subdivisions of the newly rich and middle-class bungalows begins to change the city's topography, its social strata, and its aristocratic self-image. In *The House of Lee*, the focus on the changing city and on three adapting women introduces Mrs. Atherton's continuing questions concerning the pattern of change. How does an organism, whether a person, a city, a state or a nation, that possesses an aristocratic view of itself adapt to conditions that appear to diminish its special meaning? How can anyone of rich, modest, or poor financial resources discover a self-fulfilling life purpose? Can marriage represent a stage rather than a lifelong condition of one's life? Can older women as well as older men have productive lives?

Lucy Lee Edington, the novelist's major spokeswoman, is an early fictional model of the woman executive. She handles the family's financial resources, and serves as president of the most important women's club of San Francisco and as coordinator of an organization of presidents of women's clubs that finds employment for women over forty. Still vigorous in body and mind, articulate in the current economic and political issues, and up-to-date in the arts, Mrs. Edington dramatizes the plight of sheltered middle-aged women who find themselves faced with the necessity of earning a living or of finding men to support them—the latter choice leading to a loss of their cherished independence. In a world that in 1938 is reeling between depression and a possible world war, Mrs. Edington asks how one can begin life over again. By analyzing her abilities and applying them to circumstances around her, she establishes a model of opportunity for other women that suggests that one's life goals can be adjusted at any age, and she influences her daughter and granddaughter.

Her widowed daughter, Mrs. Lee, more dependent on beauty and charm and on someone else's strength as a way of life, resists the democratizing changes around her. Like her mother attractive to men, she nonetheless prefers to remain a widow, regarding marriage as a stage in life that does not have to be perpetuated; and she selects an activity she does well— organizing bridge lessons—in order to bolster the family's resources.

Athletic, "hard-boiled" as was expected of the young generation, educated in art and literature but unprepared to support herself, Lucy Lee sometimes resents her grandmother's codes and principles, yet she too asks her grandmother's question about what to do with her changed prospects. 'Ambitious to have an interesting life, Lucy discovers that her aristocratic image of herself, based on her lineage, has caused her to live on a provincial island. Now relegated to the "white collar class," she builds her own ideal of a "realistic modern" and responsibly independent woman (p. 283). A "perfect hostess," she presides at a symbolic democratic dinner party, where the guests, representing the old and the new classes of San Francisco and the idea of a new aristocracy of achievement, exchange opinions on controversial issues. Once she proves to herself that she can earn her own living, Lucy Lee consents to marry Mark Grimthorpe, a self-made young lawyer who like Lucy comes from an "old family."

As the center of Mrs. Atherton's interest in the "psychological drama" of a woman's having to discover herself in order to imagine a new and practical mode of living her life, Lucy Edington shows her understanding of "Time's cycles." For her model of the new woman, she combines the old and the new— the ideal Virginia concept of the gentlewoman "brought up on codes and principles" and the executive woman who remains feminine though independent. Yet she is unable to reimagine her life or to create an original kind of work for herself in her new circumstances, until she overcomes her self-satisfaction in the achievements that her social position and club leadership have brought her. At this point in her evolution she must discard tradition.

Signor Santangelo, her gentleman admirer, representing European approval of the American woman, describes her efforts as a "psychological revelation." He remarks that "an

Italian woman, a Frenchwoman could have related an equally
dramatic and astonishing story, but theirs would have a theme of
love, death, or poverty," while Lucy's tale of "the tragic history
of a proud woman in search of a job" reflects a particular
American variation from the fundamental pattern of womanhood
(p. 292). Because Mrs. Edington has secured a position as a
fashion consultant which she originated for herself, she appears
more receptive to considering marriage again. In this comic
theme emphasizing practical survival with a touch of romance—
a strategy that could be a part of any stage of life—Mrs. Atherton
changes the romance heretofore favored by women readers to a
"psychological drama" of initiation (p. 293) that will extend their
knowledge of some of the realities of the changing modern
world.

Certain "flat" characters caught in the "leveling" of social
circumstances in the 1930s elaborate that drama and the theme
of the evolution of the aristocratic human spirit in a democracy.
Both men and women around the Lees dramatize the possible
effects of a decentralization of aristocratic attributes in an
individual, a social group, or a state and a nation. Miss Caroline
Ludlow, the dictatorial cousin of Mrs. Edington, who as leader of
the anachronistic "Ancient Aristocracy" of San Francisco
believes that Lucy's club work and employment deteriorate the
social structure, isolates herself from this change. In contrast, her
social peer, Aileen Banning, reverses the American dream to a
tale of riches to rags. Mrs. Banning copes with her reduced
circumstances by teaching sewing lessons in a Works Progress
Administration (WPA) project, and begins life again at fifty-six in
the movie role of Mrs. Astor, the famous social leader of New
York. This is a role that Mrs. Edington refused because she
believes that in contemporary San Francisco a society leader's
role is "no life for an intelligent woman" (p. 221). Middle-class
Nora Mahoney, self-confident and capable as executive secretary of the women's club, relieves Mrs. Edington of certain
managerial responsibilities; hence the middle class imitates the
responsibilities and leadership of the aristocratic class.

The men who admire the Lee women mirror women's
stereotypes of men, which may also project their psychological
needs in the relationship between men and women as the author
perceives them. The men as characters play the roles of the
father-confessor, the worldly-wise mentor, the lover whose

vanity allows him to be manipulated, and the successful, authoritative lover. Chiang, the Lee family's servant, who in forty years has risen to the role of "boss" of their domestic life, and Signor Santangelo, the suave and worldly gentleman, suggest that a certain dependency on a man remains part of a woman's psychic need. Twenty-four-year-old Oswald Lane, a handsome representative of the new class that imitates the elegance of life of the old aristocracy, and thirty-four-year-old Mark Grimthorpe, descendant of an old family and already a successful lawyer, respectively offer Lucy Lee the opportunity to dominate or to be willingly ruled in her relationship with a man. When, at the end of the novel, the realistic, modern Lucy Lee, desirous both of independence and of a family, capitulates to Mark's authoritative arrangement of their wedding, Mrs. Atherton appears to heal the self-conflict that has possessed most of her heroines.

The plot of the novel, typically mental and verbal, is designed to reveal the women's adaptation to necessity as they make decisions. A mystery subplot involving Chiang functions to lighten the turgidity of decision-making as a plot and to heighten the novel's rapid denouement. The women's reflections of their fears as they face the mirrors in their dressing rooms divide the novel into sequential sections devoted to each one's working out of her crisis. They lose their aristocratic provincialism as they search for their next way of living without sacrificing the ritual of dining and conversation. Their conversations center on the dangers of communism and socialism and of Hitler and Stalin, on the conflict between capital and labor, and on the rivalry between expanding Los Angeles and self-limiting San Francisco.

The varied points of view, expressed in the diction of the day, show Mrs. Atherton as an objective social historian, providing evidence that in a multi-voiced, evolving society there will be a "general leveling up as well as down" (p. 224). While Mrs. Edington observes that civilization wobbles without a wealthy class, nonetheless she predicts no "revival of social splendor until Time's cycle has completed its curve":

We shall—if we manage to avoid Socialism—have a new aristocracy— the aristocracy of intellect, talent, ability; social groups, more distinguished than the old ones, and quite as exclusive. Neither birth nor income would count; brains, accomplishment in the arts, sciences, the higher professions, a cultivation of the intellect among those denied

genius or talent, the brilliant men and women who are *doing* things.
(p. 223)

The cycle of time in *The House of Lee* demonstrates how the
aristocratic fabric of the Virginian ideal is woven into Californian
democratic inclusiveness, which recognizes individuals and
groups that achieve success through talent, intellect, and effort
as much as through birth or wealth. Gertrude Atherton views her
heroines sympathetically, allowing them individual success in
resolving their crises, while the city attempts to accommodate
itself to the spreading demands of a diverse people. She does not
develop adequately the evolving relationship between Mrs.
Edington and Signor Santangelo or between Lucy Lee and Mark
Grimthorpe. The externalized approach to their characterization does enhance her objectivity as a social panoramist of the
changing circumstances and of their effect on different types of
people and classes. The novel shows that Mrs. Atherton had kept
abreast of contemporary events and that she assimilated into her
fiction ideas and attitudes with which she may not necessarily
have agreed.[5]

III   The Horn of Life: *"I Have No Fear"*

The epigraph to *The Horn of Life* (1942), written by Gertrude
Atherton's friend, the poet Florence Hamilton, who at this time
faced blindness, suggests that this last novel of the eighty-five-
year-old novelist is concerned with discovering one's life
purpose as a strategy for confronting mortality. The novel relates
the story of Lynn Randolph, who like most of Mrs. Atherton's
heroines asks the question, Why am I born?

The action of the novel presents Lynn's experiments with the
choices open to her in a city also trying to realize its great
potential. She attempts to begin life again in San Francisco in the
1920s after three years of service as an ambulance driver in
France. She discovers not only family problems but also social
ones—Prohibition, strikes, bolshevism, the high cost of living,
and unemployment. Lynn must deal with her alcoholic, widowed
mother, with her eighteen-year-old sister Sally, a devotee of the
flapper's life, and with finding a job more fulfilling than teaching
French literature to the daughters of the wealthy. She goes into
business, tries to assist in building the future of San Francisco,

and attracts the admiration of three men. Although she feels that her potential for achievement—her "wayward gifts"—has not been fulfilled, Lynn resigns herself to "the classic Woman's Tournament"—marriage—and chooses David Adcott, a new millionaire, through whom she thinks she might be able to utilize her abilities for her city.

The novel also presents the last chapter of Mrs. Atherton's social history of San Francisco in fiction and of her characterization of her ultimate California woman as paradigms of "wayward . . . creative energies traveling around in circles and getting nowhere" (p. 294). Lynn Randolph and San Francisco have similar attributes: cosmopolitan high-headed poise, undaunted by disaster, usually competent to handle whatever happens, but not completely capable of fulfilling a great destiny. The names and personalities of Lynn's three suitors, not fully characterized, recall certain aspects of San Francisco's history and suggest appropriate grounds for a purposeful achievement of a woman and a city.

The name of T. Leland Drake, known as Tom, a devoted native son and successful businessman of San Francisco, recalls Sir Francis Drake's visit to San Francisco's harbor in 1579, and Leland Stanford, founder of Stanford University in 1886. Lynn rejects his suit because his studied blend of the old and the modern makes him predictable and stable in his actions yet incapable of responding to her moods. Sir Archibald Pryce, an urbane and distinguished Englishman, who visits long enough in the city to wish to take Lynn back to England as his wife, may imitate two Englishmen whom the author admired. Lord Bryce's view of the American commonwealth at the turn of the century inspired Mrs. Atherton's writing of *Senator North* and *The Conqueror;*[6] Pryce may also resemble Lord Northcliffe, who visited California during the era of the Graft Prosecution after the 1906 earthquake and whom the author liked because of his genial, objective appreciation of Americans. In considering yet rejecting his proposal, Lynn weighs the "uncommon lot" that she would enjoy as his wife in England against her realization that she does not love him and that marriage to him would prevent her from participating in the destiny of San Francisco.

In David Adcock, an Easterner who has become a new millionaire loyal to San Francisco, Lynn discovers a person whom she can influence and who indulges her waywardness and never

bores her. She envisions their marriage as a linkage of the values
of the East and the West that can contribute to San Francisco's
destiny. Adcock symbolizes the possibility that an outsider or a
self-made man can come to resemble a born aristocrat, like
Charles Montgomery of San Francisco society, who makes the
"best kind of democrat" (p. 131)—just as Jack Gwynne in
Ancestors proclaims that every American is an "unhatched
Englishman." In the characterization of the three suitors, Mrs.
Atherton appears to warn San Franciscans of the peril to their
full development if their city and state remain an isolated
paradise or a distant planet, unknowing and uncaring of the great
world outside.

As the culmination of her chronicle of Western civilization,
The Horn of Life recapitulates many of Mrs. Atherton's fictional
motifs. As California has stood for the United States in her story-
chronicle, so Lynn Randolph stands for a city and a questing
woman in the American procession. From her perspective in
1942, Mrs. Atherton does not see the generation after World War
I solving national, civic, and personal problems. Setting the
novel's action in San Francisco after World War I enhances the
irony of the novel's being written during World War II. She
evokes the milieu of the city—the postwar cynicism and
complacency of its citizens, the oil scandals, the horrors of
bootleg liquor, the speakeasy, the excesses of Hollywood, and
the impudent young generation. When Lynn recognizes the
delusion of her dream of being able to influence San Francisco's
destiny, she consults Joseph Loeb, the city's outstanding Jewish
leader and businessman. Reminding her of the inevitability of
boom years as well as periods of panic and depression, he warns
her that the complacent citizens of San Francisco—and
America—will not apprehend soon enough the signs of panic or
attempt to change the repetitive elements in the cycle of time.

Like Lucy Lee a new old-fashioned woman, Lynn Randolph
combines in uneasy balance the values of her Southern past and
Western present and epitomizes the dualities of nature and of
civilization. Most of Lynn's actions stem from her rationalizations
of her conflicting desires: to be independent—to do something
no woman has ever done before (p. 207)—and to have social
acceptance and companionship; to be admired by many types
and classes of people without losing her individuality; to live a
varied and novel life without indulging in the "psychic poison of

the younger generation" (p. 66); and to combine paradoxically a pessimistic and optimistic attitude toward life in recognition of human nature as it is. She decries war as an unthinking mode of achievement by individuals and by the nation. Hence she leaves a conservative purpose—teaching literature to young girls—and opens a restaurant, which she hopes will be a modern coffee house for the exchange of ideas; gives dinner parties whose middle-class and aristocratic guests converse on the issues of the day and complain of the fashion of pessimism in literature exemplified by Eliot, Pound, and Joyce (p. 206); comforts her dying mother in Hollywood; and finally and conservatively chooses marriage to Adcock.

In the 1920s, opportunities for imaginative and daring pursuits of happiness by a heroine, composed, as is Lynn, of a "bunch of antitheses" (p. 258), are limited. Though Lynn represents the independence, the self-analysis, the variables of personality of Mrs. Atherton's favorite type of woman, she also universalizes the dilemma of the imaginative, striving person, who is aware of her or his capacity for achievement but remains obscure:

What *use*—what *reason* for peculiar gifts if one was to be at the mercy of such accidents as time, environment, what not? . . . why these wayward gifts, these creative energies traveling around in circles and getting nowhere? This terrible power of conception with no hope of parturition. . . . Why . . . be born at all? (pp. 294 - 95)

After World War I, Mrs. Atherton predicted a surge of feminism in Europe and in the United states that would affect civilization and the relationship between man and woman and that would also create opportunities for the characterization of new types of characters and actions in fiction. To a certain extent she succeeds in reflecting in her fiction the choices, both necessary and free, available to women from the 1920s on. She describes more details of her heroine's daily thinking and doing, finding the "little things of life make us happy" while the greatest moments are "shadowed by fear" (p. 141). Simultaneously she presents the other side of the rampant individualism and democracy that in her opinion undermine a healthy mixing of classes and talent. In this reflection of the spreading out of opportunities, Mrs. Atherton allows Lynn Randolph to compare the contemporary novelist with the playwrights of ancient Greece, who in her opinion were the social historians of their day. Any assessment of what Mrs. Atherton has accomplished, not only in her novels of independent heroines, of the ancient world, and of famous people, must ask the critical question, Is she significant as a novelist or as a social historian or both?

IV   Golden Gate Country *and* My San Francisco: *"This Most Omniform of Cities"*

Gertrude Atherton's long connection with and intimate knowledge of San Francisco and its environs made her a logical choice for writing *Golden Gate Country* (1945) in the American Folklore Series, edited by Erskine Caldwell. Although other books in the series paid more attention to the region and its people and to the legends and social history of the area, Mrs. Atherton in her contribution to the series followed her own style of emphasizing individuals more than the region. To treat the area around the San Francisco Bay, she devotes one part to Old California and most of the three remaining parts to the mushroom growth of the city. Her impressionistic picture of the region is highlighted by vignettes of selected California personalities, by fascinating accounts of the purely human, romantic, secular, and social aspects of life in and around San Francisco, and by journalistic recording of facts on war production and women war workers. She does not attempt to present social insight or discuss the contemporary importance of the region that one might expect from such a series.

In her approach to a "wayward biography" of San Francisco, "this most omniform of cities,"[7] Mrs. Atherton chose an area of the city that could be seen with the aid of binoculars from the top of Telegraph Hill and described that scene for those who had never looked upon the city. Then she recalled impressions, memories, and experiences of San Francisco with the style of a memoir and without attention to continuity. It is a personal story of events or subjects connected with the city, such as book stores, women's clubs, banks, and slums. In a chapter titled "The Intermediate State"—which refers to an intermediate state of equal rights of men and women that Alexander the Great founded in Egypt in 332 B.C. (p. 240)—Mrs. Atherton comments on the independence of women, which had been increasing since

World War I, and provides examples of outstanding women of San Francisco. From her perspective in 1946, such examples of women's achievements, Atherton seemed to feel, vindicated her portrayal in her novels of self-reliant and talented heroines.

CHAPTER 8

A Summing Up: Gertrude
Atherton's New Aristocracy

I   Critical Reception, 1888 - 1915:
"Literary Anarchy"

FROM the publication of her first novels in 1888 and 1889, Gertrude Atherton received serious and simultaneously favorable and unfavorable critical attention, from a variety of sources. The reviews of *What Dreams May Come* and *Hermia Suydam* introduced the hallmark of her writing career—controversy. Critics employed the epithets "literary anarchy" and "intellectual anarchy" to express their puzzled surprise at her rebellious departure from the conventional and expected themes, characterizations, and methods of writing. Up to 1903, reviewers responded to her books as isolated rather than continuous artifacts of her career. Critics misapprehended her literary and thematic assumptions and her technique of spontaneity for combating what she found dull in American literature. Later critical overviews began to define the significance of that "literary anarchy" and her characterization of a different type of woman in the light of the literary and social milieu in which she wrote.

The publication of these first novels by G. Routledge, a paperback publisher in London, aroused interest among English reviewers and readers. The English poet and critic William Sharp praised *Hermia Suydam* and prophesied that Mrs. Atherton was the "coming American woman," who understood the meaning of true Realism and had the courage to depict it. For many years English praise of her work, designed in part to foster Anglo-American literary feuding, countered neglect of her work in the United States.[1] By 1897, English critics considered Mrs.

130

Atherton and Stephen Crane typically American writers, an estimate designed to stimulate the ongoing debate on the question of the superiority of English or American fiction.[2]

Reviewers of Mrs. Atherton's apprentice work in the 1890s— her California novels and short stories, the latter published primarily in British magazines—immediately identified the "deeper undercurrent of meaning" and the union of Romance and Realism that continually characterized her writing.[3] William Walsh, editor of *Lippincott's*, which serialized *The Doomswoman*, the California novel that the author considered the beginning of her career, praised the "actual vivid reality" of her California romances. When she collected her short stories in *Before the Gringo Came* (1894), reviewers described them as passionate and intense tales and as tragic episodes, particularly in the lives of women.[4] But the volume did not sell well.

Patience Sparhawk and Her Times (1897), Mrs. Atherton's first significant Realistic novel, received mixed but perceptive critical notice and triggered a negative editorial in the *New York Times*.[5] Reviewers spoke of the pervasive modernity and of the "very original talent" required to write such a long novel, while others complained about the California heroine's distorted vision of men's and women's morals and about the characters' "talk essays" which suggested the author was ridding herself of "much mental ferment."[6] The novel was banned from the Mechanics' Institute Library in San Francisco.

The three succeeding California novels drew the same mixed reception, the negative remarks focusing on the individualistic heroines, the positive on the author's refining her imagination. Reviewers of *American Wives and English Husbands* (1898) commented on the restrained power that *Patience Sparhawk* had not promised and on the contradictory traits of the loving, hating, badly spoiled heroine.[7] Readers of *The Californians*, expecting some didactic effect in the novel, objected to the less than admirable heroines and the vice-battered hero,[8] while others noted the well-told local-color details and the author's more effective control of her imaginative attempt to avoid the commonplace.[9] Reviewers generally claimed that *A Daughter of the Vine* (1899) was a disappointment in comparison with *The Californians*.[10] Then, "thinking to have some fun with the critics," Mrs. Atherton anonymously published *The Aristocrats* (1901), "a satiric presentation" of certain pretentious types of

fashionable and literary Americans.[11] The book received universal praise, some critics suspecting prominent authors, even Oscar
Wilde, as its creator—until Mrs. Atherton revealed her writing of
it.

Gertrude Atherton's twelve separate publications between
1900 and 1910, diverse in form and theme but uneven in literary
quality, in part because of her businesslike approach to
publication, enhanced her reputation. These works also
attracted mixed reviews and even elicited editorials and letters
in newspapers from readers and from the author herself. For the
first time during this decade, American and British critics
discussed her fiction in conjunction with that of other writers,
primarily with the work of women novelists and for the purpose
of assessing her literary achievement. And Mrs. Atherton's
severe and effective criticism in 1904 of William Dean Howells's
Realistic school added a different dimension to her reputation.

Deemed an unethical book by an editorial writer of the *New
York Times*, but praised for its unpopular stand against the
Spanish-American War,[12] *Senator North* (1900) was also
described as "a semi-political romance" and was contrasted with
Henry Adams's *Democracy* (1880) and with Frances Hodgson
Burnett's *Through One Administration* (1881).[13] Both British
and American reviewers acclaimed *The Conqueror, Being the
True and Romantic Story of Alexander Hamilton* (1902) as a
"bold departure" from conventional biographical and historical
methods and a "striking novelty" as a literary experiment.[14]
While several reviewers decried her partiality toward Hamilton
at the expense of Thomas Jefferson,[15] the book had many new
editions, and Van Wyck Brooks in 1952 called it "perhaps the
best of all American historical novels of the decade,
1895 - 1905."[16] Two volumes of short stories in 1902 and 1905,
whose publication might have served as an attempt to capitalize
on the popularity of *The Conqueror* and on Henry James's visit to
the United States in 1905, aroused little significant critical
comment.

Comparing Mrs. Atherton's work with that of Sarah Orne
Jewett, Mary E. Wilkins, and Ellen Glasgow, E.F. Harkins and C.
H. L. Johnston in 1901 claimed that despite the critics' insistent
ambivalence toward her writings and in spite of the variable
quality of her genius, Mrs. Atherton possessed the three most
important qualities of the novelist—to tell a story, to create

characters, and to compel the reader to read on.[17] In *The Feminine Note in Fiction* (1904), a collection of reviews on books of women writers, W.L. Courtney, reviewer of the *London Daily Telegraph*, discussed three of Mrs. Atherton's books. Courtney's preface commented on the psychological tendency of women writers to analyze and to criticize their own sex quite sharply. He acclaimed *Patience Sparhawk* as "a brilliant analytic inquiry into the baffling and scintillating paradoxes of American character," and praised Mrs. Atherton's characterizations of the tragic figure of Magdalena Yorba in *The Californians* and Alexander Hamilton in *The Conqueror*. Courtney echoed her earliest critics in praising the local-color details of her California stories, "where the perfervid civilization of San Francisco stands out in relief against the luxurious vegetation of America's original Spanish."[18]

Mrs. Atherton's four long novels added to her literary reputation but also evoked ambiguous comments on her inventiveness and characterizations and on her awkward structure and diction. Several reviewers of the widely noted *Rulers of Kings* (1904) preferred the realism of the hero's early life in the first part of the novel to the contrived, though credible, European politics and the artificial romance between the American millionaire hero and the invented daughter of Emperor Franz Joseph.[19] Other inventions in the novel—armored tanks and an electric kite to deliver explosives over enemy territory—later were called prophetic of World War I.[20] In 1954 Grant C. Knight acknowledged that in view of her description of the shallow optimism of the bourgeois reading audience, she was the only writer during 1901 - 1904 to explain sincerely and informatively to American readers "some of the intricacies and dangers of the global drive for power" of their nation.[21]

In the opinion of commentators, her longest novel and the final one in her first series in the California chronicle, *Ancestors*, offers the best measure of the strength and weakness of her artistic creed. Most of the reviews found more to praise than criticize, yet some complained about "tedious passages of analysis and discussion," about a need for correlating parts of the story with the main theme, and about her crude, unsubtle manner.[22] Others appreciated the author's frank understanding and realistic presentation of human egoism and her witty presentation of democrats and institutions (political, social, economic), all of which provoked her readers to think.[23]

Similar divided reviews greeted *Tower of Ivory* (1910), the
novel the author preferred over all, and *Julia France and Her
Times* (1912), the novel she wrote as a duty to feminism. The
New York Times reviewer remarked favorably on the latter's
being the "best suffrage book to date" because it was "a brilliant
story of modern British society."[24] One reviewer of *Perch of the
Devil* (1914) placed the characterization of its heroine beside
that of Theodore Dreiser's Carrie Meeber and Edith Wharton's
Lilly Barth,[25] while another claimed her story was told with the
narrative skill of Joseph Conrad.[26] A British critic wrote that the
incarnation of the modern western spirit in Montana in *Perch* was
a "far cry" from the mining camps of Bret Harte.[27] At the end of
1914, *California, An Intimate History* drew the quantity and
kind of acclaim given her best novels. A writer in *North
American Review* declared that in her dramatic depiction of the
state's topography and its heroes and villains "her originality is
something more than a limited gift of story telling" and is "a
paradoxical union of romance with realism."[28]

In 1909, a reviewer for the first time attempted to deal fairly
and critically with Gertrude Atherton's achievement in
American literature. Frederic T. Cooper described her "intellectual anarchy" as a unique and potent force in the nation's
literature. He noted that her strength derived from her
unillusioned view of life and from her inventing an imaginary
world that included physical baseness and moral obliquity and
frank treatment of the problem of sex. He observed that her
realistic imitation of "Nature's inscrutable way of injecting into
the intimate dreams of human life a multitude of apparently
irrelevant details" accounted for the frequent criticism of the
crude technique and uneven construction of her novels.[29]
Another holistic approach was that of John C. Underwood in
1914, who evaluated the current pale criticism of American
literature, a task that Mrs. Atherton had undertaken in her first
novels and continued in later essays when she labeled the school
of Howells as a blight on American literature. While Underwood
found merit in her assessment of the New England school, even
after he discussed her major novels from *Patience Sparhawk* to
Julia France and Her Times, he discovered nothing in her fiction
or in any followers of hers that provided an antidote. Hence,
agreeing with Cooper's estimate, Underwood concluded that as a

type of woman and as a novelist, Mrs. Atherton was a by-product
of the pressures of her age rather than a force.[30]

II Critical Reception, 1915 - 1948:
"The Panoramist, the Social Analyst"

With *Mrs. Balfame* (1916), her first mystery story, and with
her letters and articles on the war, Gertrude Atherton's
reputation as a journalist-novelist of popular and controversial
notions grew. For some reviewers, the sensational journalism
portrayed in *Mrs. Balfame* diminished the novel's effectiveness.[31]
The reviewer of the two long essays on war and feminism in *The
Living Present* (1917) claimed that Mrs. Atherton's "vigorous
and entertaining style" was not quite successful for presenting a
sociological question such as feminism in the future.[32] "Fantastic"
and the objection that it was too hasty in characterization and
theme to be credible greeted publication of *The White Morning*
(1918), her novel imagining the possible revolt of German
women against the Kaiser's government.[33]

After the relatively poor reception of Mrs. Atherton's three
postwar novels utilizing California material for the first time
since *Ancestors* in 1907, *Black Oxen* (1923) and its theme of
rejuvenation restored her literary reputation. As a mystery story,
The Avalanche (1919) was thought superior to *Mrs. Balfame*; two
critics wrote that *The Sisters-in-Law* (1921) suffered from a lack
of "holding power" though its feminine psychology was clever;
and *Sleeping Fires* (1922), valued for its picture of San Francisco
in the 1870s, seemed as faded as an old-fashioned tract on
alcoholism.[34]

Reviewing *Black Oxen*, Henry Seidel Canby praised both its
scientific hypothesis and its logical conclusion and the brilliant
and panoramic description of the well-to-do class of New York in
the 1920s, within which Mrs. Atherton depicted well-defined
groups interacting with each other and symbolic of a breakdown
of an exclusive society. However, despite her themes of time's
ravages and of a questioning of life purpose, Canby declared that
the novelist lacked the flowing, rhythmic style of Edith
Wharton's rendition of New York, as well as a great novelist's
sympathy with the hidden sources of life that would permit her
to achieve "that simple utterance which revealed human

nature."[35] Nonetheless, *Black Oxen* generated varied attention. It was banned from the library of Rochester, New York, and the author argued before the New York State Legislature in 1923 against censorship of books on the basis of isolated words or phrases deemed obscene for young readers by the Clean Books League.[36] Even three years after the publication of *Black Oxen*, Mrs. Atherton disclosed that she could not count the number of letters that she had received from readers wishing for the rejuvenation of her heroine, many of them working women with families wanting to enjoy work with their original zest and to escape the ravages of "ruthless nature."[37] Not so successful with its popularly understood Freudian theme, *The Crystal Cup* (1925) was declared by critics, among them H. L. Mencken, to be pseudoscience and fantastic psychology.[38]

Mrs. Atherton's three historical novels depicting the Periclean age and the legend of Dido and Aeneas received critical acclaim from university professors as well as from reviewers for their historical and archaeological fidelity, and depiction of scenes, but only faint praise for narrative power and felicity of expression. On *The Immortal Marriage* (1927), the reviewer in the British *Spectator* spoke of its careful writing and construction, but missed in it "one touch of divine fire which would kindle it into life"; whereas Professor Paul Shorey claimed the novel was a better history of Greece than that of H. G. Wells or Spengler.[39] A "competent" and "excellent" historical novel, said two critics of *The Jealous Gods* (1928),[40] while one reviewer apprehended Dido as a feminist and another as a "human as well as a tragic figure."[41] Mrs. Atherton's story of Augustan Rome seven years later, *Golden Peacock* (1936), also drew similar diverse remarks—commendation for its recreation of Rome's atmosphere, for a more fluent and colloquial style than in *The Immortal Marriage*, and for a portrayal of a certain fundamental unity in the human spirit by its hinting at the similarity of problems in Rome and in the contemporary United States.[42]

Between 1915 and 1930, interviewers as well as professional book reviewers considered Gertrude Atherton a lively and controversial source of opinion on literature and public issues. Their articles, questioning her on Howells, on English and American fiction, on feminism, war, and bolshevism, produced no connected view of her fiction and repeated the commonplaces of criticism concerning her works. But they also added some fine points to her literary reputation. Among these, "Pendennis,"

Isabel Paterson, Lionel Stevenson, and Joseph Henry Jackson could perceive a consistent intention in Mrs. Atherton's writing. "Pendennis" elicited a definition of Mrs. Atherton's types of characters as progressive and predictive of the future because the author's ironical view of human nature rejected the sentimental "blinders" of the *Atlantic* and the "blue goggles" of the Addisonian *Spectator*.[43] Isabel Paterson in 1924 attempted to explain the influence of Mrs. Atherton's personality and ironic views on her work as a cause of what some critics called the uneven quality of her style and the structure of her novels.[44] In "Atherton Versus Grundy, The Forty Years' War" (1929), Lionel Stevenson undertook a more complete critical study of Mrs. Atherton's controversy and achievement. He described as "melodramatic realism" the quality that sustained her novels despite the criticism of her types of characters, of her unconventional themes, and of the sometimes sordid, unheroic back alleys of life that she depicted. Stevenson claimed that "her strident tone [diction as well as style and subject matter] is justified in that a mellower tone would not have aroused even a semblance of independent thinking on the part of the readers."[45] Like Paterson, Joseph Henry Jackson described Gertrude Atherton as a social historian, part journalist, part fictionist, watching the parade of humanity on Main Street and peering into windows and souls of men and women along the way.[46]

Mrs. Atherton's autobiography, *Adventures of a Novelist* (1932), attracted wide critical attention in both England and the United States, while only mild interest was shown in her other publications in the 1930s. The reviewers of the autobiography nearly unanimously acclaimed her "candor" and "detached criticism" in regard to herself, her friends and acquaintances, and her literary adventures and social life.[47] Most reviewers appeared more interested in what her adventures and social contacts, especially in London in the 1890s, revealed about the personality of the author than in their pertinence to a clear understanding of her fiction.

Perhaps because of the war, Gertrude Atherton's last two novels and her two books on the history and personalities of the San Francisco area received only minor attention. Joseph Henry Jackson's twenty-page essay utilized a review of *The House of Lee* (1940) to present an overview of the novelist's works and to appraise her as "the panoramist, the social analyst, the independent, even recklessly challenging writer she has always been."[48]

Other reviewers noted her "verve" in voicing a conservative and "piercing plaint" on issues such as the Depression, labor, the New Deal, and pinkies through the words of three generations of California women.[49] A reviewer of *The Horn of Life* (1942) commented on the lack of irony in the story of a conventional young woman and a complacent city, but perceptively linked the story and the recurrence of war.[50]

From 1930 on, critical opinion of Gertrude Atherton's work appeared in brief references in articles and in books of literary history and criticism. In articles that in 1930 and 1931 examined California writers, Carey McWilliams and Charles C. Dobie respectively chided Mrs. Atherton for "writing fustian" and praised her writing "The Randolphs of Redwoods" (1883), the first Realistic novel to come out of the Pacific coast area.[51] Historians of the novel usually defined Mrs. Atherton's achievement only by her early California material, by her depiction of women's concerns, and by her limited effect on Realism through her criticism of Howells. While Fred Lewis Pattee's *The New American Literature, 1890-1930* identified Mrs. Atherton with Edith Wharton as an aristocrat and a transitional writer, Arthur Hobson Quinn's *American Fiction, An Historical and Critical Survey* (1936) placed Mrs. Atherton's volumes "distinctly below" those of Owen Wister.[52] Like Pattee, H. H. Hatcher isolated his discussion of women novelists in a separate chapter, and recorded the timeliness of Mrs. Atherton's themes of social history and feminism and her provocative attack on them as evidence of the diverse energy of the modern novel.[53] Only her California novels and stories clamed the attention of Ernest E. Leisy in *The American Historical Novel;* he called *The Conqueror* "fictionized biography" and omitted reference to the novels of ancient Greece and Rome.[54]

III *Critical Reception after 1948: Summary Visions*

A critical ambivalence—whether to treat Mrs. Atherton's achievement in relation to her personality or to her literary intention—has continued since her death in 1948. Henry James Forman in 1961, relating details of her life as a "brilliant California novelist," perceptively mentioned her sensitive ability to absorb impressions and experiences and to observe with detachment all the processes of living; she possessed a capacity of inclusiveness and detachment that Forman declared "the great geniuses" such as Shakespeare, Dante, and Goethe possessed.[55] In "Gertrude Atherton, Daughter of the Elite," in *Americans and the California Dream, 1850 - 1915*, Kevin Starr endeavored to place Mrs. Atherton's first nine California novels in the social and cultural milieu of the state and of San Francisco, and he decided that she was a novelist only because she wrote novels.[56] Elinor Richey returned to the cult of personality as criticism in her essay, "The Flappers Were Her Daughters, The Liberated, Literary World of Gertrude Atherton,"[57] while Carolyn Forrey linked Mrs. Atherton's new woman to the cultural, social, and psychological milieu of women in the late nineteenth century.[58]

B. R. McElderry, Jr., arguing that Atherton's story "The Bell in the Fog" (1905) contained her fictional warning to Henry James that his artistic achievement had been won at too great a price—alienation from his country and from his earlier reading public—[59] provides a clue for further critical understanding of Mrs. Atherton's intention and achievement. Her perception of the basic question of human life—happiness as the purpose of living—was anchored firmly in the inherited spirit and culture of Western civilization as both were extended in the New England, Southern, Midwestern, and Western experience in the United States and as she perceived them. As she observed the effects of heredity and environment on her own cyclical journey away from and back to California and on that of her characters, so have recent scholars begun to examine the significance of her observations, thus correcting in part earlier criticism that explained her work primarily in the light of conventional literary expectations. Gail Thain Parker, discussing William Dean Howells in respect to Realism and feminism, has contended that both Gertrude Atherton in her fiction and the nineteenth-century suffrage leaders sensed that Howells's kind of realism was inimical to woman's self-development.[60] In her study of Mrs. Atherton's novels of the 1890s and their appeal to readers, Sybil Weir similarly concluded that the author's expression of feminism—the struggle of her heroine to become a woman independent of her society's conventional expectations—was limited by her extolling home and family as the one acceptable goal for her heroines.[61]

IV   *Critic of the Pursuit of Happiness*

Gertrude Atherton believed that the main purpose of life is to be happy. Yet she did not change her naming as a "fool's paradise" an individual's egotistic pursuit of a narrow happiness or an arcadian state's retreat into complacency or its drive toward arrogant and exclusive power. She explored the influences of heredity and environment on the development of people and nations in order to define the good influences in both and to expose the evils and weaknesses of relying on one or the other exclusively. Her significant women and men characters—Isabel Otis and Jack Gwynne, Ida Compton and Alexander Hamilton—modified the disadvantages and advantages of the conditions of their early lives through deliberately thoughtful rebellion and trial and error. Her early heroines needed men to approve of their new combination of intellect, will, and sensuality. As women gained self-confidence and experience within and beyond woman's conventional role, they became teachers and supporters of each other, even mentors of men, without losing their charm and their desire for a loving but companionable relationship with a man at some stage in their lives. Their extended consciousness, related from a woman's point of experience, added to the growing trend in the novel's psychological realism.

Gertrude Atherton's feminism and her insistence on a fulfilling relationship between a man and a woman as a condition of happiness have been misunderstood. She condemned whatever she found in the lives of men and women which made their lives complacent, sterile, and monotonous. She laid the blame for the interrelatedness of the ennui of women, the tyranny of men, and the parental abuse of power over children on the cultivated social roles and attitudes that separated individuals from their own internal rhythms and from nature's rhythms.[62] She wrote her fiction to show the tragedy involved in the complacent waste of human possibilities in any age in any level of society, and especially in a virgin and expanding nation such as the United States. Hence she portrayed a necessary general "leveling up and down" within and among traditional divisions of society that were based on birth, education, and wealth, a movement that she predicted would create a new aristocracy consisting of all individuals who had developed their ability and talent. To Mrs.

Atherton, the novel's fluid form seemed analogous to the variety of ways that types of characters could pursue happiness appropriate to their inner natures and outer circumstances. To her, the union of Romance and Realism permitted her to characterize actual types of personalities who desired adventure and knowledge of the peaks and valleys of life.

Gertrude Atherton never wholly followed an ideology lodged in a continuum of an aristocracy of birth and *noblesse oblige* and a democracy of opportunity for unequal ability and talent. Early she observed that the distance between the rich and the poor in California stemmed in part from aristocratic land holdings. Her memory of the decline of her social fortune because of her family's loss of land later led her to sympathize somewhat with the premises of socialism. Yet her significant heroines recognized that socialistic control of human energy and ambition would produce the ennui similar to that caused in part by the traditional division of labor and responsibility based on class and sex. So she located the greatest possibility of expanding the human spirit, particularly of women, in the encouragement of individual talent at the expense of merely fulfilling traditional roles. Hence she changed a conventional motive of a certain kind of novel from a love story to a psychological drama.

She knew that many women could outgrow the complacency and submissiveness associated with women's traditional role, and she indicated the possibilities of change through the interaction of intelligence, imagination, physical activity, work, and femininity, as she showed in her characterizations of Isabel Otis, Mrs. Edington, and Lucy Lee. If she and her heroines attacked the evils of a commercial, materialistic culture that acted like a civilization, or if they objected to the leveling of the American bloodstream by Oriental and middle and southern European immigration, they offered not a magic formula of retreat to Arcadia but a challenge to individuals to carry out their duty to develop fully wherever or under whatever circumstances they found themselves.

In that Gertrude Atherton saw the possibility of a "fool's paradise" residing in any region, not only in California, and not only in an individual's undeveloped ego but in social and ethnic groups with narrow perspectives on their part in and responsibility toward the race, she transcended time and place. Only as she used San Francisco and her California heroines as models of

progress and development can she be thought of as a regional
writer. Her major interest in a region lay in a universal inner or
psychological one, a place where identity begins and expands
outward if and when social, political, and economic conditions
foster expansion. Hence Mrs. Atherton is a social historian,
making critical observations on a civilization that are based on
her own assumptions of the relationship between human nature
and culture. The first part of her novels realistically explained
nature and civilization as her characters saw them, and the last
part imaginatively and romantically joined nature and the human
spirit in an endeavor to transcend human limitations. She spoke
out, sometimes crudely and undecorously but wittily from her
point of view, on the lighter and darker sides of life for the
benefit of her readers' knowledge of the great world. She wrote
of human beings as she saw them, and she tried not to judge them
but to let the reader apprehend the peaks and valleys of human
existence.

Notes and References

Chapter One

1. Some of the materials on which the chronology and the biographical portions of this study are based are found in Mrs. Atherton's *Adventures of a Novelist* (New York, 1932); page numbers in parentheses in this chapter, unless otherwise specified, refer to that book. The novelist's papers and correspondence pertaining to the first fifty years of her life were lost in the San Francisco earthquake and fire in 1906, but later biographical materials have been collected in the Gertrude Atherton Papers in Bancroft Library, University of California, Berkeley; in the Library of Congress and in several other university libraries; and in an unpublished manuscript of the memoirs of Florence Atherton Dickey of Santa Rosa, California, granddaughter of Mrs. Atherton.

2. The scandal resulting from alcoholism allegedly occurred in the George Gordon family, prominent from 1850 to 1879. Mrs. Atherton's story of 1883 and her revision of it in 1899 were fictional transformations of a scandal accepted as gossip or truth in those years. See Albert Shumate's *The California of George Gordon* (New York, 1976) for a historian's view.

3. Cyril Clemens, "Gertrude Atherton," *Overland* 90 (October 1932), 239. See "One Bad Book," *New York Tiimes*, September 29, 1900, p. 648 (an editorial on *Senator North*), answered by Mrs. Atherton in the *New York Times*, October 6, 1900, p. 660.

4. *Adventures of a Novelist*, p. 426.

5. Fred Lewis Pattee, *The New American Literature, 1890 - 1930* (New York, 1930), p. 247.

6. Mrs. Atherton's correspondence with Minnie Maddern Fiske from March 16, 1897, to December 31, 1912, can be found in the Fiske Papers, Library of Congress.

7. Stoddart Papers, Library of Congress.

8. See, for example, Gertrude Atherton, "The American Novel in England," *Bookman* 30 (February 1910), 633 - 40.

9. Henry James, "American Letter," *Literature* 2 (April 30, 1898), 511; *Literature* 2 (April 9, 1898), 422 - 23; also in *Henry James, The American Essays*, ed. Leon Edel (New York, 1956), pp. 204 - 208, 218 - 19.

10. "The Reason Why the Novelist [Henry James] Has Now a Boom," *Argonaut* 55 (February 6, 1905), 92.

11. See B. R. McElderry, Jr., "Gertrude Atherton and Henry James," *Colby Library Quarterly* 3 (November 1954), 269 - 72.

12. Gertrude Atherton, "Why Have We Not More Great Novelists?" *Current Literature* 44 (February 1908), 158 - 60.

13. See "Gertrude Atherton's Answer to Ellen Glasgow," *New York Sun*, Literary Section, April 15, 1916, p. 1.

14. "A Word from the Author of *Senator North*," *New York Times Saturday Review*, October 6, 1900, III, p. 660.

15. *Patience Sparhawk* (London and New York, 1897), pp. 252 - 53. See *Tower of Ivory* (New York, 1910), p. 144, where a catalog of writers aids in point of view and characterization.

16. Gertrude Atherton, "The Novel: Its Friends and Foes: A Reply," *Bookman* 14 (October 1901), 137 - 38.

17. See "Why Have We Not More Great Novelists?"; Joyce Kilmer, "American Novel Is Flamboyant and New England Tradition, Though Venerated, Is a Blight," *New York Times*, July 25, 1915, pp. 18 - 19; Gertrude Atherton, "Some Truths About American Readers," *Bookman*, 18 (February 1904), 658 - 60.

18. "The American Novel in England," 633 - 40.

19. Gertrude Atherton, "The Alpine School of Fiction," *Bookman* 55 (March 1922), 26 - 33.

20. Gertrude Atherton, *The House of Lee* (New York, 1940), p. 293.

Chapter Two

1. "Why Is American Literature Bourgeois?" *North American Review* 175 (May 1904), 771 - 81; "Wanted: Imagination," *What Is a Book?*, ed. Dale Warren (Boston, 1935), pp. 43 - 60. Page numbers in parentheses in this chapter, unless otherwise specified, refer to *Adventures of a Novelist*.

2. See also "Gertrude Atherton Assails 'The Powers,'" *New York Times*, December 29, 1907, VI, p. 2.

3. "The Woman of Truth at Last Will Turn," *New York Times*, September 30, 1915, p. 10.

4. "A Word from the Author of *Senator North*," p. 660.

5. "Why Is American Literature Bourgeois?" p. 780.

6. Quotations in this paragraph are taken from "Why Is American Literature Bourgeois?" and "Gertrude Atherton Assails 'The Powers.'" Mrs. Atherton appears to have admired Bret Harte's succinct characterizations and Mark Twain's ability to flavor a realistic analysis of society with such romance as the reader wanted.

7. *What Dreams May Come* (Chicago, 1888), pp. 63, 65 - 66; *Hermia Suydam* (New York, 1889), pp. 30 - 31.

8. "Illustrious Seconds," *North American Review* 148 (June 1889), 771.

9. "Why Is American Literature Bourgeois?" p. 780.

10. "Gertrude Atherton Assails 'The Powers,'" p. 2; "Why is American Literature Bourgeois?" p. 791.

11. "The Novel and the Short Story," *Bookman* 17 (March 1903), 36.

12. "Wanted: Imagination," pp. 51 - 54. Mrs. Atherton alludes to John Galsworthy to illustrate a writer's "truly magnificent craftsmanship" (p. 51).

13. Kilmer, "American Novel," p. 18.

14. "A Word from the Author of *Senator North*," p. 660.

15. "Pendennis" [pseudonym], "Novels, Novelists, and Reviewers," *New York Times*, April 16, 1905, III, p. 3.

16. "What the Day's Work Means to Me," *Bookman* 42 (February 1916), 693.

17. William E. Harris, "Gertrude Atherton," *Writer* 39 (March 1929), 62.

18. "Wanted: Imagination," p. 57.

19. "The Woman of Tomorrow," *Yale Review*, n.s. 2 (April 1913), 412 - 35.

20. "A Word from the Author of *Senator North*," p. 660.

21. *The Sisters-in-Law* (New York, 1921), p. 340.

22. Foreword in Charles Caldwell Dobie, *Less Than Kin* (New York, 1926), pp. vii - ix.

23. "What the Day's Work Means to Me," pp. 691 - 95.

24. "The Woman of Tomorrow," pp. 412 - 35.

25. "Affinities," *Overland*, second series, 51 (January 1908), 4 - 7.

26. "Present Unrest Among Women,"*Delineator* 74 (August 1909), 118; "The Woman in Love," *Harper's Bazar* 43 (December 1909), 1179 - 81; 44 (January 1910), 46 - 48; 44 (May 1910), 304 - 305, 342.

27. See *The Sisters-in-Law*, p. 240, where the phrase, "romantic realism," is linked to a possible tragedy in the halcyon California environment.

28. See W. L. Courtney, *The Feminine Note in Fiction* (London, 1904), pp. 115 - 34; Lionel Stevenson, "Atherton Versus Grundy: The Forty-Years' War," *Bookman* 69 (July 1929), 464 -72.

29. It was conventional for novels to be written in parts at this time because of the prospect of serialization in magazines.

30. "Few Expect Novel Typifying America," *New York Times*, March 16, 1916, p. 13.

31. "Wanted: Imagination," p. 43. See also her list of types of writers in "The Woman At Last Will Turn," *New York Times*, September 30, 1915, p. 10.

32. "The Young Person as a Novel-Reader," *Critic*, n.s. 19 (February 11, 1893), 86 - 87. Mrs. Atherton testified at censorship hearings in New

York State in 1923 involving attempts to protect young people (*New York Times*, April 19, 1923, p. 1).
33. "Wanted: Imagination," p. 58.
34. See especially "Some Truths About American Readers," pp. 658 - 60.
35. "Pendennis," "Novels, Novelists, and Reviewers," p. 3.
36. Ibid.
37. "May Sinclair's Biographical Novel," *New York Times Book Review*, September 7, 1919, p. 445.
38. Henry James, "The Question of Opportunities," *Literature* 2 (March 26, 1898) 356 - 58, rpt. *Henry James: The American Essays*, pp. 197 - 204.
39. "The Novel: Its Friends and Foes," pp. 137 - 38.
40. "The Young Person as a Novel-Reader," p. 86.
41. "Why Is American Literature Bourgeois?" p. 775.
42. "Gertrude Atherton Assails 'The Powers,' " p. 2; "Literary Merchandise," *New Republic* 3 (July 3, 1915), 223 - 24.
43. "Novels, Novelists, and Reviewers," p. 3.
44. *The Women Who Make Our Novels* (New York, 1918), p. 44.
45. Stevenson, "Atherton Versus Grundy," p. 471; Kevin Starr, *Americans and the California Dream, 1850 - 1915* (New York, 1973), p. 364.
46. "What the Day's Work Means to Me," p. 693.
47. "Wanted: Imagination," p. 44.
48. Ibid., p. 45.
49. Hippolyte Taine, "Introduction," *History of English Literature*, tr. H. Van Laun (New York, 1886), pp. 1 - 21.
50. "Wanted: Imagination," p. 46.
51. "Pendennis" [pseudonym], "My Types—Gertrude Atherton," *Forum* 58 (November 1917), 585 - 94. See Paul John Eakin, *The New England Girl* (Athens, Ga., 1977), for a discussion of the disparity between interpretation of fictional heroines and the reality which they represented in the works of Hawthorne, Stowe, Howells, and James.
52. Ibid., 594.
53. See *A Whirl Asunder* (New York, 1895), p. 16, and *A Daughter of the Vine* (London, 1899), p. 16.
54. "The Woman of Tomorrow," p. 431.
55. Ibid., p. 421.
56. "Is There a Moral Decline?" *Forum* 65 (March 1921), 27; "Why Have We Not More Great Novelists?" p. 159.
57. Twenty-five years later, Mrs. Atherton contributed a chapter, "Chains of the Past," to a similar composite novel, *The Woman Accused* (New York, 1933).
58. "Why Have We Not More Great Novelists?" p. 159.

59. *A Whirl Asunder,* pp. 83ff.

60. Herbert Spencer, "The Philosophy of Style," *Essays: Moral, Political, and Esthetic* (New York, 1890), pp. 9 - 47.

61. Isabel Paterson, "Gertrude Atherton—A Personality," *Bookman* 58 (February 1924), 638.

62. Francis W. Halsey, *Women Authors of Our Day in Their Homes* (New York, 1903), p. 254.

63. "Some Truths About American Readers," p. 658.

64. Halsey, p. 254.

65. "Wanted: Imagination," pp. 59 - 60.

Chapter Three

1. Page numbers in parentheses in this chapter, unless otherwise specified, refer to *Adventures of a Novelist* or to the book under discussion in each section.

2. In her dedication of the book to Bourget, Gertrude Atherton declared, in part: "the ultimate religion of that strange composite known as The American, is Individual Will. . . . The final result may be a race of harder fibre and larger faculties than any in the history of civilization. That this extraordinary self-dependence and independence of certain traditions that govern older nations make the quintessential part of the women as well as of the men of this race I have endeavoured to illustrate in the following pages."

3. In *The Feminine Note in Fiction,* Courtney remarks that the author's delineation of Patience's varied adventures suggests that Mrs. Atherton did not appear to like her heroine very much (p. 116).

4. The characterization of Patience in these respects antedates Kate Chopin's Edna Pontellier in *The Awakening* (1899) by two years. Ernest Earnest in *The American Eve: Fact and Fiction, 1775 - 1914* (Urbana, Ill., 1975) documents the discrepancy between the actual sexually and intellectually aware American woman and the innocent figure of women in American literature.

5. *New York Times Saturday Review,* October 15, 1898, p. 686; also in *Bookman* 8 (November 1898), 254.

6. "American Letter," *Literature* 2 (April 30, 1898), 511 - 12. "The Question Among the Novelists," *Literature,* 2 (April 9, 1898), 422 - 23.

7. *Athenaeum,* 3680 (May 7, 1898), 597.

8. Ibid.

9. Gertrude Atherton, "Divorce in the United States," *Contemporary Review* 72 (September 1897), 410 - 15.

10. " Affinities," pp. 4 - 7.

11. Frederick Taber Cooper, *North American Review* 186 (December 1907), 609.

Chapter Four

1. *Adventures of a Novelist,* p. 452. Page numbers in parentheses refer to the work under discussion in each section, unless otherwise specified.
2. Ibid., pp. 298 - 99, 304, 306.
3. Ibid., p. 307; *Senator North,* pp. 17, 73.
4. Larzer Ziff, *The American 1890s: The Life and Times of a Lost Generation* (New York, 1966).
5. *New York Times Saturday Review,* October 6, 1900, p. 660.
6. D. A. Randall and J. T. Winterich, "*The Conqueror:* Collations... Notes, " *Publishers' Weekly* 140 (November 15, 1941), 1927.
7. Gertrude Atherton, "The Hunt for Hamilton's Mother," *North American Review* 175 (August 1902), 229 - 42.
8. *New York Times Saturday Review,* April 19, 1902, p. 265.
9. *Providence* [R.I.] *Sunday Journal,* April 6, 1902, p. 15.
10. Pattee, p. 247.
11. *Adventures of a Novelist,* p. 447.
12. Ibid., p. 362.
13. Ibid, pp. 447, 560.
14. Ibid., pp. 393, 465 - 68.
15. Ibid., p. 471.
16. Ibid., pp. 494 - 95.
17. Frederick Taber Cooper, *Bookman* 40 (November 1914), 310 - 11.

Chapter Five

1. James D. Hart, *The Popular Book: A History of America's Literary Taste* (New York, 1963), p. 233. Page numbers in parentheses in the text refer to *Black Oxen* unless otherwise specified. ›
2. H. L. Mencken, "The Gland School," *American Mercury* 6 (November, 1925), 249 - 51.
3. *Adventures of a Novelist,* p. 578.
4. Gertrude Atherton, "Second Youth, The Latest in Reactivation," *Liberty,* July 8, 1939, pp. 17 - 18, 20. Dr. Harry Benjamin, *Rejuvenation,* with an introduction by Norman Haire (London, 1937).
5. "Wanted: Imagination," p. 43; Joseph Henry Jackson, "Watch the Parade, Write It All Down," *San Francisco Chronicle,* November 1, 1942, p. 10.
6. *Adventures of a Novelist,* pp. 556 - 57.
7. See "Dr. Steinach Coming to Make Young Old," *New York Times,* February 9, 1922, p. 28; "Rejuvenation by Surgery," February 26, 1922, VI, p. 10; "Rejuvenation Is Filmed," October 9, 1923, p. 17.

8. *Adventures of a Novelist*, p. 556.

9. Gertrude Atherton, "Love Is Not All," *Harper's Bazaar* 60 (January 1926), 89.

10. Henry Seidel Canby, "Mrs. Atherton's 'Black Oxen,'" *Definitions: Essays in Criticism*, Series 2 (New York, 1924), pp.237-41.

11. *Black Oxen*, copyright by Associated First National Pictures, Inc., 1923.

12. Charles Hanson Towne, "Mrs. Atherton's Scoop," *Bookman* 56 (February 1923), 762.

Chapter Six

1. *Adventures of a Novelist*, pp. 498 - 500. Page numbers in parentheses in the text refer to the novel under discussion unless otherwise specified.

2. "Wanted: Imagination," p. 54.

3. *Adventures of a Novelist*, p. 568.

4. Quotations in this paragraph are from *Adventures of a Novelist*, pp. 569 - 70, 577, and 341.

5. "Alcibiades," *Times Literary Supplement*, November 29, 1928, p. 933.

6. Frances L. Robbins, "The Week's Reading," *Outlook* 153 (November 13, 1929), 427 - 28; "Fiction Briefs," *Nation* 130 (January 18, 1930), 51.

7. *Adventures of a Novelist*, pp. 341 - 42.

Chapter Seven

1. *Adventures of a Novelist*, p. 578. Page numbers in parentheses refer to the book under discussion in each section unless otherwise specified.

2. Isabel Paterson, ". . .Yesterday," *Yale Review* 22 (Autumn 1932), 192.

3. Of Henry James's conversation, the novelist remarked: "there were times when he could be as clear and direct and coherent as Edmund Gosse or any other noted conversationalist. . . . He talked as if every sentence had been carefully rehearsed; every semicolon, every comma, was in exactly the right place, and his rounded periods dropped to the floor and bounced about like tiny rubber balls" (*Adventures of a Novelist*, p. 285).

4. See "Books . . . All Kinds," *New Yorker*, April 16, 1932, pp. 64 - 65.

5. N. L. R., Review of *The House of Lee*, *Saturday Review of Literature* 22 (October 5, 1940), 19 - 20.

6. *Adventures of a Novelist,* pp. 309 - 10, 449 - 50.

7. Preface, *My San Francisco, A Wayward Biography,* pp. 7 - 8.

Chapter Eight

1. *Adventures of a Novelist,* pp. 147, 165.

2. "The Lounger," *Critic,* n.s. 27 - 28 (June 26, 1897), 444

3. Ella Sterling Mighels, *The Story of the Files* (California, 1893), p. 349; William Walsh, "Mrs. Atherton's Novels: A Dialogue," *Lippincott's* 50 (September 1892), 412 - 15.

4. "Talk About Books," *Chautauquan* 20 (November 1894), 254. "Fiction," *Literary World* 25 (October 20, 1894), 352.

5. Editorial, *"Patience Sparhawk and Her Times:* Critics Answered," *New York Times,* May 15, 1898, p. 18.

6. "Fiction of the Season," *New York Times Saturday Supplement,* May 15, 1897, p. 4; "Chronicle and Comment," *Bookman* 5 (May 1897), 194; "Novel Notes," *Bookman* [London] 12 (April 1897), 18.

7. "American Wives and English Husbands," *Bookman* 7 (May 1898), 251; "Recent Novels," *Spectator* 80 (March 26, 1898), 450 - 51; "Literature," *Critic* n.s. 29 (May 14, 1898), 328 - 29.

8. *"The Californians,"* *Critic,* n.s. 30 (November 1898), 394 - 95; "Books of the Week," *Outlook* 60 (October 24, 1898), 537.

9. William M. Payne, "Recent Fiction," *Dial* 25 (November 1, 1898), 305; "Novel Notes," *Bookman* 8 (November 1898), 253 - 54.

10. "Recent Fiction," *Critic,* n.s. 32 (July 1899), 648; "Recent Novels," *Independent* 51 (August 17, 1899), 2230 - 31.

11. *Adventures of a Novelist,* pp. 316 - 39.

12. Gertrude Atherton's reply, *New York Times,* October 6, 1900, p. 660. Editorial, " ...'One Bad Book,' " *New York Times,* September 29, 1900, p. 648; William M. Payne, "Recent Fiction," *Dial* 29 (September 1, 1900), 126; *"Senator North,"* *Bookman* [London] 19 (November 1900), 58.

13. "A Semi Political Romance," *New York Times,* June 9, 1900, p. 371; Stephen L. Gwynn, "Fiction and Politics," *Edinburgh Review* 193 (January 1901), 168 - 72.

14. James Douglas, "Three Lady Novelists," *Bookman* [London] 22 (July 1902), 133 - 34; J. P. Mowbray, "That 'Affair' of Mrs. Atherton's," *Critic* 40 (June 1902), 501 - 505.

15. William M. Payne, "Recent Fiction," *Dial* 32 (June 1, 1902), 385; Walter S. Edwards, "Gertrude Atherton's 'The Conqueror,' " *Bookman* 15 (May 1902), 255 - 56.

16. Van Wyck Brooks, *The Confident Years, 1885 - 1915* (New York, 1952), p. 214.

17. E. F. Harkins and C.H.L. Johnston, *Little Pilgrimages Among*

Women Who Have Written Famous Books (Boston, 1901), pp. 205 - 21.

18. Courtney, *The Feminine Note In Fiction* (London, 1904), pp. 115 - 34.

19. "Rulers of Kings," *Times Literary Supplement,* April 15, 1904, p. 116; William M. Payne, "Recent Fiction," *Dial* 37 (July 16, 1904), 40.

20. J. E. Boulton, Letter, *New York Times,* September 22, 1916, p. 6; Helen Bullis, Letter, *New York Times,* September 6, 1914, V, p. 376.

21. Grant C. Knight, *The Strenuous Age in American Literature* (Chapel Hill, N.C., 1954), pp. 64 - 68.

22. William M. Payne, "Ancestors," *Dial* 43 (November 16, 1907), 317 - 18; "Current Fiction," *Nation* 85 (October 24, 1907), 377; Frederick T. Cooper, "Ancestors," *North American Review* 186 (December 1907), 607.

23. *Athenaeum* 4178 (November 23, 1907), 650; "Atherton Novel Awakens Thought," *New York Times,* October 26, 1907, p. 676.

24. "For Woman Suffrage, Mrs. Atherton's New Novel," *New York Times Book Review,* April 21, 1912, p. 239.

25. Frederick T. Cooper, "Some Novels of the Month," *Bookman* 40 (November 1914), 310 - 11.

26. "Books of the Autumn," *Independent* 80 (November 16, 1914), 243.

27. "Perch of the Devil," *Spectator* 113 (September 19, 1914), 399.

28. "New Books Reviewed," *North American Review* 201 (January 1915), 93 - 94.

29. Frederick T. Cooper, "Gertrude Atherton," *Bookman* 30 (December 1909), 357 - 63.

30. John C. Underwood, *Literature and Insurgency: Ten Studies in Racial Evolution* (New York, 1914), pp. 391 - 446.

31. "Current Fiction," *Nation* 102 (March 16, 1916), 313.

32. "New Books Reviewed," *North American Review* 206 (October 1917), 635 - 37.

33. Springfield *Republican,* March 10, 1918, p. 3; "The New Books," *Outlook* 118 (February 20, 1918), 297; "Notes on New Fiction," *Dial* 64 (February 28, 1918), 205.

34. E. F. Edgett, *"The Avalanche,"* Boston Transcript, February 19, 1919, p. 8; R. D. Townsend, "Midwinter Fiction," *Outlook* 127 (February 16, 1921), 267; "Fiction," *ALA Booklist* 17 (March 1921), 217; H. W. Boynton, *"Sleeping Fires,"* New York Evening Post, February 25, 1922, p. 447.

35. Canby, *Definitions,* pp. 237 - 41.

36. Editorial, "Removal of *Black Oxen* in Rochester," *New York Times,* October 4, 1923, p. 22. Editorial, "Topic of the Times," *New York Times,* March 20, 1923, p. 20; Editorial, "The Worst Bill Yet," *New York Times,* April 18,1923, p. 20; "Likely to Railroad Clean Book

Bill," *New York Times,* April 19, 1923, p. 1.

37. "Love Is Not All," p. 148.

38. Henry L. Mencken, "The Gland School," *American Mercury* 6 (November 1925), 245 - 51; "Sex and Pseudoscience in a Psychic Novel," *New York Times Book Review,* August 30, 1925, p. 14; *"The Crystal Cup," Times Literary Supplement,* September 10, 1925, p. 582.

39. "Fiction," *Spectator* 139 (July 16, 1927), 104; Paul Shorey, "Breviora...*The Immortal Marriage,*" *Classical Philology* 22 (July 1927), 332.

40. L. P. Hartley, "Alcibiades," *Saturday Review* 147 (January 26, 1929), 20; "Biography and Fiction Briefs," *Nation* 127 (December 12, 1928), 665 - 66.

41. Margaret Wallace, *"Dido," New York Evening Post,* November 9, 1929, p. 11; Frances L. Robbins, "The Week's Reading," *Outlook* 153 (November 13, 1929), 427 - 28.

42. Joseph L. French, "Horace's Niece," *Commonweal* 24 (May 22, 1936), 111; Lorine Pruette, *"The Golden Peacock," New York Herald Tribune Books,* April 12, 1936, p. 12; Lee E. Cannon, "Rara Avis," *Christian Century* 53 (May 6, 1936), 673.

43. "Pendennis," "My Types—Gertrude Atherton," *Forum* 58 (November 1917), 585 - 94.

44. Isabel Paterson, "Gertrude Atherton, A Personality," *Bookman* 58 (February 1924), 632 - 37.

45. Lionel Stevenson, "Atherton Versus Grundy, The Forty Years' War," *Bookman* 69 (July 1929), 464 - 72.

46. Joseph Henry Jackson, "Watch the Parade, Write It all Down," *San Francisco Chronicle,* November 1, 1942, p. 10.

47. "A Novelist's Memoirs," *Times Literary Supplement,* September 15, 1932, p. 635; Arthur Colton, "Mrs. Atherton's Life," *Saturday Review of Literature* 8 (May 28, 1932), 754; Mary Ellen Chase, "A Bright Lady," *Commonweal* 16 (July 27, 1932), 334.

48. Joseph Henry Jackson, *Gertrude Atherton* (New York, 1940), p. 20.

49. N. L. R., *"The House of Lee," Saturday Review of Literature* 22 (October 5, 1940), 20; Ramona G. Cook, *"The House of Lee," Boston Transcript,* October 5, 1940, p. 5.

50. Olive B. White, "Fiction," *Commonweal* 37 (December 25, 1942), 259.

51. Carey McWilliams, "The Writers of California," *Bookman* 72 (December 1930), 352; Charles C. Dobie, "The First California Authors," *Bookman* 72 (February 1931), 591.

52. Fred Lewis Pattee, *The New American Literature, 1890 - 1930* (New York, 1930), pp. 245 - 48; Arthur Hobson Quinn, *American Fiction: An Historical and Critical Survey* (New York, 1936), pp. 505 - 06.

53. H. H. Hatcher, *Creating the Modern American Novel* (New York, 1935), p. 87.

54. Ernest H. Leisy, *The American Historical Novel* (Norman, Okla., 1950), pp. 141 - 42.

55. "A Brilliant California Novelist, Gertrude Atherton," *California Historical Society Quarterly* 50 (March 1961), 1 - 10.

56. Starr, *Americans and the California Dream, 1850 - 1915*, pp. 345 - 64.

57. Elinor Richey, "The Flappers Were Her Daughters, The Liberated Literary World of Gertrude Atherton," *American West* 11 (July 1974), 4 - 10, 60 - 63.

58. "Gertrude Atherton and the New Woman," *California Historical Society* 55 (Fall 1976), 194 - 209.

59. Bruce R. McElderry, Jr., "Gertrude Atherton and Henry James," *Colby Library Quarterly* 3 (November 1954), 269 - 72.

60. "William Dean Howells, Realism and Feminism," *Uses of Literature*, Harvard English Studies 4 (Cambridge, Mass., 1973), pp. 133 - 61.

61. Sybil Weir, "Gertrude Atherton and the Limits of Feminism in the 1890s," *San Jose Studies* 1 (February 1975), 31.

62. "The Woman of Tomorrow," pp. 412 - 35.

Selected Bibliography

PRIMARY SOURCES

1. Novels (Listed in chronological order of first printing).

What Dreams May Come. By 'Frank Lin." Chicago, New York: Belford, Clarke and Company, 1888.

Hermia Suydam. New York: Current Literature Company, 1889.

Los Cerritos, A Romance of the Modern Time. New York: John W. Lovell Company, 1890; Ridgewood, N.J.: The Gregg Press, 1968.

A Question of Time. New York: John W. Lovell Company, 1891.

The Doomswoman. New York: J. Selwin Tait, Sons, 1893; Upper Saddle, N.J.: Literature House, 1970.

Before the Gringo Came. New York: J. Selwin Tait, Sons, 1894.

A Whirl Asunder. New York, London: Frederick A. Stokes Company, 1895.

Patience Sparhawk and Her Times. London, New York: John Lane, The Bodley Head, 1897; Upper Saddle, N.J. Literature House, 1970.

His Fortunate Grace. New York: D. Appleton and Company, 1897.

The Californians. London: John Lane, 1898; Ridgewood, N.J.: The Gregg Press, 1968.

American Wives and English Husbands. London: Service and Paton, 1898.

The Valiant Runaways. New York: Dodd, Mead and Company, 1898.

A Daughter of the Vine. London, New York: John Lane, The Bodley Head, 1899.

Senator North. New York, London: John Lane, The Bodley Head, 1900; Ridgewood, N.J.: The Gregg Press, 1967.

The Aristocrats, Being the Impression of Lady Helen Pole During Her Sojourn in the Great North Woods as Spontaneously Recorded in Her Letters to Her Friend in North Britain, the Countess of Edge and Ross. London, New York: John Lane, 1901; Ridgewood, N.J.: The Gregg Press, 1968.

The Conqueror, Being the True and Romantic Story of Alexander Hamilton. New York, London: The Macmillan Company, 1902.

The Conqueror, A Dramatized Biography of Alexander Hamilton. Revised. New York: Frederick A. Stokes Company, 1916.

Mrs. Pendleton's Four-in-Hand. New York, London: The Macmillan Company, 1903.

155

Rulers of Kings. New York, London: Harper & Brothers, 1904. *The Traveling Thirds.* London, New York: Harper & Brothers, 1905.

Rezánov. New York, London: Authors and Newspapers Association, 1906; Upper Saddle River, N.J.: Literature House, 1969.

Ancestors. New York: Doubleday, Page & Company, 1907.

The Gorgeous Isle. New York: Doubleday, Page & Company, 1908.

Tower of Ivory. New York: The MacMillan Company, 1910.

Julia France and Her Times. New York: The Macmillan Company, 1912.

Perch of the Devil. New York: Frederick A. Stokes Company, 1914.

Before the Gringo Came: Rezánov and *The Doomswoman. New York:* Frederick A. Stokes Company, 1915.

Mrs. Balfame. New York: Frederick A. Stokes Company, 1916.

The White Morning. New York: Frederick A. Stokes Company, 1918.

The Avalanche, A Mystery Story. New York: Frederick A. Stokes, 1919.

Transplanted. New York: Dodd, Mead and Company, 1919.

The Sisters-in-Law, A Novel of Our Time. New York: Frederick A. Stokes, 1921.

Sleeping Fires. New York: Frederick A. Stokes Company, 1922.

Black Oxen. New York: Boni & Liveright, 1923.

The Crystal Cup. New York: Boni & Liveright, 1925.

The Immortal Marriage. New York: Boni & Liveright, 1927.

The Jealous Gods, A Processional Novel of the Fifth Century B.C. (Concerning One Alcibiades). New York: Horace Liveright, 1928.

Dido, Queen of Hearts. New York: Horace Liveright, 1929.

The Sophisticates. New York: Horace Liveright, 1931.

Golden Peacock. Boston, New York: Houghton Mifflin Company, 1936.

The House of Lee. New York, London: D. Appleton - Century Company, 1940.

The Horn of Life. New York, London: D. Appleton - Century Company, 1942.

2. Short Story Collections

Before the Gringo Came. New York: J. Selwin Tait, Sons, 1894.

The Splendid Idle Forties, Stories of Old California. New York, London; The Macmillan Company, 1902; Ridgewood, N.J.: The Gregg Press, 1968.

The Bell in the Fog and Other Stories. New York, London: Harper & Brothers, 1905; New York: Garrett Press, 1968.

The Foghorn. Boston, New York: Houghton Mifflin Company, 1934; Freeport, N.Y.: Books for Libraries, 1970.

Splendid Idle Forties. Kentfield, Calif.: Allen Press, 1960.

3. Miscellaneous Writings.

A Few of Hamilton's Letters, ed. Gertrude Atherton. New York, London: The Macmillan Company, 1903.

California, An Intimate History. New York, London: Harper & Brothers, 1914; New York: Boni & Liveright, 1927; New York: Blue Ribbon Books, 1935; Freeport, N.Y.: Books for Libraries, 1971.

Life in the War Zone. New York: Systems Printing Company, 1916.

The Living Present. New York: Frederick A. Stokes Company, 1917.

Adventures of a Novelist. New York: Liveright, 1932.

Can Women be Gentlemen? Boston: Houghton Mifflin Company, 1938; Freeport, N.Y.: Books for Libraries, 1970.

Golden Gate Country. New York: Duell, Sloan & Pearce, 1945.

My San Francisco, A Wayward Biography. Indianapolis, New York: Bobbs-Merrill Company, 1946.

4. Articles Pertinent to Her Writing

"Illustrious Seconds," *North American Review* 148 (June 1889), 769 - 71.

"The Young Person as a Novel-Reader," *The Critic,* n.s. 19 (February 11, 1893), 86 - 87.

"Literary London," *Bookman* [London] 16 (June 1899), 65 - 67.

"The Novel: Its Friends and Foes: A Reply," *Bookman* 14 (October 1901), 137 - 38.

"The Novel and the Short Story," *Bookman* 17 (March 1903), 36 - 37.

"Some Truths About American Readers," *Bookman* 18 (February 1904), 658 - 60.

"Why Is American Literature Bourgeois?" *North American Review* 175 (May 1904), 771 - 81.

"The New Aristocracy," *Cosmopolitan* 40 (April 1906), 621 - 27.

"Affinities," *Overland Monthly,* Second Series, 51 (January 1908), 4 - 7

"The Woman in Love," *Harper's Bazar* 43 (December 1909), 1179 - 81; 44 (January 1910), 46 - 48; 44 (May 1910), 304 - 305, 342.

"The American Novel in England," *Bookman* 30 (February 1910), 633 - 40.

"The Woman of Tomorrow," *Yale Review,* n.s. 2 (April 1913), 412 - 35.

"What the Day's Work Means to Me," *Bookman* 42 (February 1916), 691 - 95.

"Is There a Moral Decline?" *Forum* 65 (March 1921), 26 - 33.

"The Alpine School of Fiction," *Bookman* 55 (March 1922), 26 - 33.

"Love Is Not All," *Harper's Bazaar* 60 (January 1926), 89, 148.

"Wanted: Imagination," *What Is A Book? Thoughts about Writing,* ed. Dale Warren. Boston: Houghton Mifflin Company, 1935.

SECONDARY SOURCES

CANBY, HENRY S. *Definitions,* Series 2. New York: Harcourt, Brace, 1924, pp. 237–41, on *Black Oxen.* Praises Atherton's making

credible a unique situation and her social panorama of New York.
COOPER, FREDERIC TABER. "Gertrude Atherton," *Bookman* 30 (1909),
    357-63; also in *Some American Story Tellers.* New York: Holt,
    1911, pp. 245-64. Frankly examines her sources of writing ability
    and material, her intention and her literary achievement to date.
COURTNEY, W. L. *The Feminine Note in Fiction.* London: Chapman &
    Hall, 1904, pp. 115-34. Historically interesting early observations
    on Atherton's work, expecially *Patience Sparhawk and Her Times*
    and *The Conqueror.*
FORMAN, HENRY JAMES. "A Brilliant California Novelist, Gertrude
    Atherton," *California Historical Society Quarterly* 40 (1961),
    1-10. Informal appreciation of Atherton and her writings.
FORREY, CAROLYN. "Gertrude Atherton and the New Woman,"
    California Historical Quarterly 55 (1976), 194-209. Perceptive.
    Links Atherton's biography with the novelist's projection of
    women characters seeking fulfillment through a broader participa-
    tion in life.
HARRIS, WILLIAM E. "Contemporary Writers, XI—Gertrude Atherton,"
    Writer 39 (1929), 62-64. Presents Atherton's ideas, expressed in an
    interview, on imagination, writing fiction, and types of writers.
JACKSON, JOSEPH HENRY. *Gertrude Atherton.* New York: Apple-
    ton-Century [1940]. Reviews Atherton's long writing career as he
    discusses *The House of Lee* (1940). Identifies Atherton the writer
    as part journalist and part fictionist.
———. "Watch the Parade; Write It All Down," *San Francisco
    Chronicle,* November 1, 1942, p. 10. Presents familiar biographical
    details; predicts eight of her novels will be valuable to social
    historians as sources of mores of San Francisco from 1860s to 1940.
KNIGHT, GRANT C. *The Strenuous Age in American Literature.* Chapel
    Hill, N.C.: University of North Carolina Press, 1954, pp. 64-68.
    Admires Atherton's little-known *Rulers of Kings* (1904) for its
    competent and prophetic portrayal in a period of the strong man of
    some intricacies and dangers of a nation's drive for power.
McCLURE, CHARLOTTE S. "Gertrude Atherton (1857-1948)," *American
    Literary Realism* 9 (1976), 95-101. A bibliographical essay.
———. "A Checklist of the Writings of and About Gertrude Atherton,"
    American Literary Realism 9 (1976), 103-62. The most complete
    bibliography to date.
———. *Gertrude Atherton.* Western Writers Series. Boise, Ida.: Boise
    State University Press, 1976. Emphasizes Atherton's California
    fiction and nonfiction as both regional and universal in theme.
———. "Gertrude Atherton's California Woman: From Love Story to
    Psychological Drama, *Itinerary 7 Criticism.* Bowling Green, Ohio:
    Bowling Green University Press, 1978, pp. 1-9. Examines Ather-
    ton's creation of a new type of heroine in order to narrate the

journey or quest of a woman for a full and varied life.

McELDERRY, BRUCE R. JR., "Gertrude Atherton and Henry James," *Colby Library Quarterly* 3 (1954), 269-72. Argues that in the short story, "The Bell in the Fog" (1905), Henry James is not only the hero but is warned that his artistic successes have been won at the price of his alienation from his native land and from "the most vital springs of his own earlier genius."

MOWBRAY, J. P. "That 'Affair' of Mrs. Atherton's," *Critic* 40 (1902), 501-505. Criticizes the uncritical glorification of Alexander Hamilton in Atherton's *The Conqueror*.

OVERTON, GRANT M. "Gertrude Atherton," *The Women Who Make Our Novels.* New York: Moffat, Yard, 1918, pp. 41-53. A reviewer of books as a newsworthy occurrence, Overton confronts the critical controversy over Atherton's themes, style, and structure by identifying the novelist's antipathy toward literary schools, her fulfillment of her audience's desire for narrative action and no moral end, and her description of an adaptable and evolving woman.

PARKER, GAIL THAIN. "William Dean Howells: Realism and Feminism," *Uses of Literature*, Harvard English Studies, No. 4, ed. Monroe Engel. Cambridge: Harvard University Press, 1973, pp. 133-61. Provocative. Argues that Atherton, along with suffragists Elizabeth Cady Stanton and Frances Willard, recognized an enemy of feminism in the Realistic heroines in Howells's fiction and presented their own Romantic models of aspiring women.

"PENDENNIS." "My Types—Gertrude Atherton," *Forum* 58 (1917), 585-94. Discusses the sources of Atherton's types of characters, her use of irony, the short story, and the effect of war on literature.

RICHEY, ELINOR. "The Flappers Were Her Daughters: The Liberated, Literary World of Gertrude Atherton," *American West* 11 (1974), 4-10, 60-63. Combines biographical details with references to critical and popular opinion of Atherton's works.

SINCLAIR, UPTON B. *Money Writes!* London: T. Warner Laurie, 1931; St. Clair Shores, Mich: Scholarly Press, 1970, pp. 74-80, 103, 108. Identifies Atherton's conflict between aristocratic values and middle-class mores and discusses *Black Oxen* from a Socialist viewpoint.

STARR, KEVIN. "Gertrude Atherton, Daughter of the Elite," *Americans and the California Dream, 1850-1915.* New York: Oxford University Press, 1973, pp. 345-64. Starr assesses Atherton's story-chronicle of the social history of California as a "minor, but interesting contribution."

———. "The Last of the High Provincials," *California Living Magazine*, September 19, 1976, pp. 37-43. Interesting comparison of Gertrude Atherton's and Kathleen Norris's "imaginative identification" with San Francisco in their fiction.

STEVENSON, LIONEL. "Atherton Versus Grundy: The Forty Years' War," *Bookman* 69 (1929), 464-72. Attempts to account for the controversy over Atherton's books and for her successful reaction to critical opposition; examines certain significant elements in Atherton's mind that produce her diversity of theme and method as well as her frequently inappropriate diction and turgid style.

UNDERWOOD, JOHN CURTIS. "Mrs. Atherton and Ancestry," *Literature and Insurgency, Ten Studies in Racial Evolution.* New York: Kennerley, 1914, pp. 391-446. One of the first critical attempts to explore the meaning of Atherton's novels in American literature. Deals with the assumptions that underly the intellectual anarchy in her fiction.

VAN VECHTEN, CARL. "Some 'Literary Ladies' I Have Known," *Yale University Library Gazette* 26 (1952), 97-116. Informal memories of a friend.

WALSH, WILLIAM S. "Mrs. Atherton's Novels, A Dialogue," *Lippincott's Magazine* 50 (1892), 412-15. Comments on Atherton's early combination of Romance and Realism and gives a surprisingly favorable review of *Hermia Suydam* (1889).

WEIR, SYBIL. "Gertrude Atherton: The Limits of Feminism in the 1890s," *San Jose Studies* 1 (1975), 24-31. Excellent. Examines the relationship of Atherton's analysis of attributes ascribed to women in the 1890s to her characterization of fictional women, and suggests the limits that the female reading audience placed upon her characterizations of men and women.

Index